MENTORING THE NEXT GENERATION

Make a Lasting Difference

By

Dr. R. Peter Mason with Dr. Dino Pedrone

PRESS

Mentoring the Next Generation

by Dr. R. Peter Mason with Dr. Dino Pedrone

Printed in the United States of America

ISBN 9781624197321

www.xulonpress.com

Dedication

Mentoring the Next Generation expresses our passion to make a lasting difference.

Therefore, we dedicate this book to our grandchildren.

Rhett Mason

Ryder Mason

Chase Gough

Courtney Gough

Mia Pedrone

Ella Oster

Olivia Oster

May our lives help them come to know and serve the Lord Jesus Christ!

Table of Contents

Introduction

We are passionate about equipping the next generation to be leaders in the Church. We have witnessed and experienced God using the mentoring process to make a lasting difference in our own lives and the lives of others.

I (Peter) am the grandson of a Swedish carpenter. I learned how to build homes as Grandpa Pearson's apprentice. At 10 years old, I was sweeping sawdust off the floor of a house under construction and picking up stones before seeding the lawn.

When I was a high school student Grandpa handed me the paint and paintbrush and said, "Paint the sash of the window."

I asked, "Where's the masking tape?"

Grandpa said, "Real painters don't use masking tape." Then he walked away. Those were the days before spray painting and vinyl windows!

Grandpa trusted me and encouraged me to develop skills for building homes. Soon my brothers and I were framing, roofing and siding homes in his absence.

Not only was carpentry Grandpa's job, it was his calling. His passion to provide "starter" homes for young families inspired me. He equipped me with building skills that helped me work my way through school. I still enjoy working around the house with Grandpa's tools. His example and lessons often come to mind.

Historically, uncles, older cousins and grandfathers have been the primary source of mentors for young men. Aunts and grandmothers mentored young women. My own life and ministry have been strongly influenced by mentors. Has yours? Every area of my theological understanding, character development and skill in ministry is the product of a core of individuals who built into my life. Mentoring relationships nurture personal development. My friend, Dr. Dino Pedrone, has spent a lifetime modeling mentoring.

I (Dino) am not sure where the time has gone! I have been busy in ministry. Forty of those years as a pastor and now I have the privilege of being the president of a school that I deeply love. Davis College in the Greater Binghamton, New York area for over 100 years has been training men and women to go into the ministry. I love what I do and, in fact, have deeply loved the years that God has allowed my wife and me to serve our Lord.

I still believe that the greatest days of our ministry are ahead. But I must also be realistic. I am looking back on more years than I will be looking ahead. Now as I look back there is an obvious question that needs an answer. The question is, "What will I leave behind?" There are those articles in our home that we will leave to our family, some money to people we love and Christian organizations, but what else? For me, it is the lives that I have impacted in both formal and informal ways through mentoring. On a regular basis I receive words of thanks from those who have come into my life and by the grace of God a connection happened that made that a difference. It was more than leading them to Christ! It was the investment in their lives.

As a pastor I remember the many things that I did. There were sermons to preach, visits to make, various meetings, hospital visits, and a plethora of things that needed to be accomplished. Now that I look back the most valuable thing I did took place over a cup of coffee, or a trip to the hospital with a young man wanting to learn, or traveling to speak at a conference and sharing the time with someone. Mentoring ... it is caught as much as it is taught!

At the college that I am privileged to oversee, I regularly tell our students to come to my office and chat or I go to the Broadway Café located on our campus to find a surprised student to chat with. I travel weekly to churches to speak and, frankly having lunch with the pastor and his wife after church is some of the most valuable time I spend as we often talk about ministry. Transparent time spent in real life situations provides huge teachable moments. Some of these moments make an eternal difference.

Our encouragement to women and men everywhere is to invest in people's lives. It may be in a formal setting or it may be in a relaxed atmosphere. The fulfillment it brings is unbelievable. You will impact people and some of them are individuals you never realized. It is a passion of mine and as you see it developed in your life you will see how it fulfilling it is.

Why are mentoring relationships so important? The Bible reveals that God in his very nature is a relational being. He is the triune God existing in three persons. Therefore, he has always existed in relationship. Close connection is a fundamental truth of existence, the very foundation of the likeness of God.[1]

Knowing God is the most important relationship. After we are reconciled to him through His Son, he desires that we have fellowship with one another. Mentoring is one kind of human relationship that has been acclaimed as "the highest point on a continuum of relationships."[2] Essential to effective growth through mentoring is a close relationship of trust. Mentoring, as a relational process of personal development, is rooted in the very nature of God and his created order.

The time is going by for us. It is for you too! Those things you have learned need to be shared with someone who needs you in their life. Be a mentor for God's glory and you will find fulfillment. The satisfaction is huge and the blessings are numerous! This book will be a help! Read it. Apply the teaching. And, enjoy encouraging others through mentoring!

Part 1

Making a Difference

CHAPTER ONE

The Motivation for Mentoring

An old idea has renewed interest. The transfer of conviction, character and skill through mentoring relationships is as timely today as it was in the days of the Bible. What is it that commends the biblical practice of mentoring in our day?

Fragmented Family

We live in a "fatherless America." The family is increasingly divided by divorce and separation. Most children of divorced couples live with their mothers. Other fathers are absent due to the expectations of work. Still other dads are physically present, but emotionally distant. In other cases illness limits a father's involvement. My (Peter) own dad suffered from a debilitating neurological illness that limited his participation in some aspects of my life. As a result, in high school I sought out the input of other mature Christian men to mentor me.

Without parental involvement, a young person is deprived of a model to follow, an anchor to hold, and a fence to guide in life. Because of fragmentation, the family cries out for mentors who are willing to invest in the next generation.

Because of dysfunctional families, young people do not know how to resolve conflict. They see conflict in the home result in divorce rather than resolution. They see church conflict result in firing the pastor rather than reconciliation. Youth see disagreement in the political arena result in name calling rather than constructive bipartisanship. *Mentoring can provide stability and positive role models for young people from fragmented families.*

Mobility

A new job opportunity brings a call for the moving van. As a result, the nuclear family is geographically separated from the extended family. Bobb Biehl, founder of Mentoring Today, writes, "The mobility of our society makes for a widespread rootless feeling and disconnected relationships. Close family members frequently live five hundred to five thousand miles apart. This leaves most of us hundreds or thousands of miles from aunts and uncles who in times past would naturally have become our mentors."[3]

Historically, an uncle was an ideal mentor for a young man and an aunt mentored a young woman. They reinforced the convictions of home. They cheered on a younger person and provided an example to follow. *Mentoring can provide an extended family in an age of mobility.*

Gender Identity

Howard Hendricks, a Christian Education professor at Dallas Theological Seminary, was once asked, "What has been your greatest contribution as a seminary professor?" In response he answered, "To affirm the maleness of many of my students."[4]

We are in a society that is increasingly confused concerning masculinity and femininity. Our culture has created role confusion and identity crisis. Bobb Biehl has observed:

> About 30 percent of the male Christian leaders I work with struggle with issues about their manhood. They ask questions such as: 'What is a man? How does a boy become a man? When does he know he's a man? Am I a man? How do I know I'm a man?' A mentoring relationship can provide the opportunity for manhood to emerge, to be discussed, to be defined, and to be entered into with a level of confidence that would rarely be possible without a mentoring relationship.[5]

Defining masculinity in terms of specific tasks like mowing the lawn or repairing the plumbing is culturally conditioned. The days of identifying cooking and washing the dishes as "woman's work" is passé.

Dr. Larry Crabb in *Enjoying the Difference* provides a perspective on masculinity and femininity. Masculinity, he suggests, is expressed in a man's created nature to advance into the world to make a difference. A man enters his world with purpose. However, he needs to be deeply valued and respected for his efforts to handle these responsibilities of life. He is strengthened by the encouragement of mom and dad. He values the supportive companionship of his wife. He appreciates the mentor who cheers him on.

In contrast, a woman focuses on relational closeness—a sense of attachment and security. Essential to her core identity is the need to nourish relationships, to deepen attachments and to enter a relational network. A man's need is for respect and admiration in accomplishing a task. A woman's need is for protection and security in relationship.

Mentoring can provide an effective masculine and feminine identity in an age of confusion.

Technological Changes

We have moved from an agrarian society through the industrial age into the age of information. Over fifty percent of the U.S. economy is now devoted to communication. Due to this computer technology, many new businesses are starting in homes. This development is impacting relationships because most friendships develop at work. With technology comes isolation. People are becoming more and more lonely. In a high-tech culture mentoring provides connection to keep life in balance. *Mentoring can provide high-touch relationships amidst a high-tech culture.*

Accountability

George Barna, a Christian pollster, presented a seminar entitled "What Effective Churches Have Learned." His research has found that "born again" Christians are uninformed concerning fundamental biblical truths, uninvolved in their churches and unethical in their moral practices. He defined as "born again" those who say they have "made a personal commitment to Jesus Christ that is relevant today" and affirm "they would go to heaven based on a personal relationship with Jesus Christ."

Shockingly, according to Barna, sixty-percent of "born again" Christians say "there is no such thing as absolute truth." Two out of five of those who are "evangelizing" others say: "A good person can earn salvation" and one quarter say, "Jesus Christ sinned." Thus, many of those who share the "Gospel" do not even understand the fundamentals of the Gospel!

From Barna's research it is evident that we are in need of accountability in the church. Who will help a young people mature in their faith? Who will help them develop a biblical world-view, godly character, and skills in life? We need increased accountability within the Church regarding our biblical convictions and the messages that we send to non-Christians. *Mentoring is ideally suited to meet this pressing need for accountability.*

Leadership Development

Our churches are in critical need of effective leadership. Many gifted Christian leaders have forsaken the use of their gift within the Church because in that context they are overworked and under-appreciated.

Too many churches do not prepare future leaders. Their nominating committees may hastily look through the church directory in their annual search for leaders. This evaluation of potential leaders is often superficial.

Of those churches that prepare leaders, too many training programs meet in the classroom and focus only on the textbook. Too many Bible schools and seminaries have been preparing Bible teachers and preachers without leadership training.

Leadership development must include biblical teaching accompanied by character training and ministry practice. Modeling and coaching by a skillful mentor is particularly appropriate in equipping for a real world—and a real church—leadership role. *Mentoring is a critical link in the preparation, protection and empowering of Christian leaders for the new millennium.* Wouldn't you find the recommendation of a respected mentor concerning a potential leader a more compelling reference than the diploma from an academic institution?

> Mentoring is a critical link in the preparation, protection and empowering of Christian leaders for the new millennium.

Effective Communication

The busters (born from 1965-83), and the millennium kids (born from 1984-2002), respond to relational communication more than reasoned linear instruction. The younger generation insists, "Show me what your beliefs look like! Live out your convictions! Be authentic!"

Growing up in an environment of religious syncretism and moral relativism, young people respect truth that is practiced. They respond to truth shared through relationship—incarnational truth. *Mentoring can communicate effectively across generational lines as mentors model their message.*

Friendless Male

> **The Bible presents mentoring as an effective and frequently used method of discipleship and leadership development.**

Men in America have been called "the friendless male." We live in an individualistic and increasingly mobile culture in which relationships, especially between men, do not develop with frequency or depth. One survey found that less than five percent of men have a "best friend." Personally, I find it challenging to cultivate close friendships with other men. I highly value the friendships I have.

Why does the church softball team have such dedicated players? Why are the pickup trucks lined up in front of the local diner at 6 A.M. before work? Why is the downtown sports bar filled on Monday evening? Why did a million men gather to "stand in the gap" in the nation's capital? In part, it is because men need and value relationships with other men.

There is a significant need for men to cultivate relationships. The most important relationship is with God himself. Men also need godly relationships with other men. *Mentoring can build bridges of friendship for the friendless male.*

Multigenerational Churches

Many church leaders are seeking to cultivate multigenerational churches. However, senior saints feel out of touch with the new generation, and young people feel uninvited into the core decision-making of the church. What better way to unify and strengthen the church than through mentoring!

Mature members can invest time and experience into the lives of younger members. How about taking a young man with you for that next tee time? How about inviting a young woman to share a time over coffee as you share your wisdom as an experienced mom? Young people can express their appreciation for mature believers by asking for their wise perspective. *Mentoring can bridge the generation "gap" in multigenerational churches.*

Biblical Principles

The Bible presents mentoring as an effective and frequently used method of discipleship and leadership development. Having reviewed the examples in the Scriptures, we believe mentoring is a normative method of training. Mentoring was not simply a process of instruction that ancient cultures practiced. This pedagogy is effective throughout history and across cultures. Throughout this book we will look at biblical examples of mentoring. We will glean from these examples principles for mentoring effectively.

Examples of Mentoring

The wind was gusting. It was the first week of February, 1970. I (Dino) had just accepted the call to pastor The Open Door Church in Chambersburg, Pennsylvania .I stood between the downtown buildings of the education wing and the church auditorium. The wind caused the door to loosely tap the church building. I drew my collar up around my neck. It was cold. The door opened and there stood a woman whom I met when I was the candidate for the pastoral position at the church two weeks prior. I remembered her well.

"Pray for my husband", she said. "He is going to be a preacher!"

She then proceeded to tell me that he was unsaved. I thought to myself that this was an enormous order. He had not accepted the Lord yet and she wanted him to be a preacher. There she stood and behind her was a man who seemed to bashfully peak around the shoulder of his wife.

"This is my husband", she announced. "He accepted Christ last week and now he is going to be a preacher!"

I looked at him and he barely spoke and there was an obvious shock expressed on his face at the thought of being a preacher. He later told me in his very quiet unassuming manner that he had no intention of being a preacher.

As any young preacher would do I wanted to see our church grow. Being the ripe age of 24 years I had great ambitions and enthusiasm with little understanding of how to do it. I decided to have a visitation program. In the '70's, visiting in homes and sharing the gospel was an excellent way to reach people. I made the announcement that I wanted our church to have a strong visitation program. I encouraged our church membership to meet at the church on a Thursday night and to go out on visitation.

Little did I know how intimidating this was to people. The first night of visitation I arrived early and set up several tables with visitation cards, tracts, flyers of the church, and numerous other items from mints to door hangers! Unfortunately no one came. The next week I spent several minutes in the announcement section of our service explaining the importance of the visitation program. The next Thursday night I went through the same process and this time I brought my wife. We doubled our crowd. Two came. My wife and I!

I decided there must be another way to deal with this subject. I had learned D. James Kennedy's Evangelism Explosion plan of salvation, the Romans' Road and various parts of the Four Spiritual Laws. I felt I could easily show others how to win someone to the Lord. I told our small congregation that I would now be looking for volunteers to go with me. I had one volunteer. The dear lady who told me that her husband would be a preacher had explained to her husband he should volunteer and he did. His name was Art. Hers was Frieda. He had little education. In a stumbling set of few words he explained to me that he would go with me. So I took him simply because there was no one else. I was disappointed. Little did I realize that this would be a huge lesson to me about mentoring and I would be the one to learn!

I took my friend with me. We went week after week. On some occasions we were able to sit and talk to someone in the confines of their homes. Once in a while someone accepted Christ as their Savior. My friend, Art, began to meet with me for coffee. He was full of questions. He carried his Bible the way I carried it. When we were in a home he followed along in the scriptures the same as I did. One evening I was sitting on the ottoman and shared the gospel with a couple as they relaxed on their couch. I noticed they kept looking toward my friend who sat behind me. I wondered what he was doing. When I showed them a verse in the Bible I glanced back to see what he was doing. He had his testament open and he was talking under his breath to no one!

In future weeks upon entering a home I carefully and discretely recommended that Art sit in a corner of the room and then he could do whatever he wished. He would be out of the sight of those who I was talking with. Without my knowledge he was following everything I did. He went to conferences with me. He went to places that I would preach.

Then came the day! I did not think this day would happen and frankly I did not want it to happen. Art, in his humble and quiet way told me that he was ready to do the talking in a home as we went on visitation. I knew in my heart I would need to help him. Although he had studied, was prepared, and willing I was not sure how this event would go.

I taught Art to ask the EE question initially. "If you were to die today do you know you are going to heaven?' It is a simple yet profound question. That evening we went to a home and a man who looked like he could play middle linebacker for a professional football answered the door. After a few moments of pleasantries Art popped the question. But in his nervousness he confused it and said, "If you were to die today do you know how to go to heaven or how to go to hell!!" I thought for sure we would be asked to leave. The man said no and called his entire family. They went at Art's request to the dining room table and there was a seat for the man's wife, four sons and Art but not me. I sat in the corner of the living room (much like I had placed Art all those weeks) and watched the proceedings. I thought Art did a very poor presentation of the gospel. At the end he led the entire family to Christ. All six of them accepted the Lord!

That night as we were driving away I had my little Ford Maverick. I had never led six people to Christ. Art looked at me and sheepishly said, "We never did lead six people to Christ, did we? Did I do all right?" I responded, "Not bad…your first time out!" The next week he led three more to Christ and in a few weeks he was instrumental in bringing to the church 222 people, many of whom accepted the Lord.

Recently I returned to the town. It was Art's home going service. I drove by the old church property. The church is relocated and sits today on a beautiful fifty-five acre campus. The old building is gone. The educational building remains. I looked and remembered a dear woman saying, "My husband will be a preacher." Art did get ordained and at this home going service there were many who told of the many he led to Christ.

The last time I saw Art was on the Davis College campus. I will never forget his last word to me. Art, not a hugger, gave me a hug and said "Take it easy boss. Thanks for being my mentor." That was it. In a few weeks he went to heaven!

That was one of my first mentoring experiences. I was not even aware through much of the experience what was happening. There are very few things more rewarding than those words. "Take it easy boss. Thanks for being my mentor."

Howard Hendricks has made a significant impact on understanding and applying mentoring. We can't find a more compelling motivation for mentoring than his personal story. He writes:

> I was born into a broken home in the city of Philadelphia. My parents were separated before I was born. I never saw them together except once— when I was called to testify in divorce court. I'm sure I would have been reared, died, and gone to hell, and nobody would particularly have cared, except that a small group of believers got together in my neighborhood to start an evangelical church. That small group of individuals developed a passion for their community.
>
> Walt belonged to that church, and he went to the Sunday School superintendent and said, "I want to teach a Sunday School class."
>
> The superintendent said, "Wonderful, Walt, but we don't have any boys. Go out into the community. Anybody you pick up—that's your class."

I'll never forget the day I met him. Walt was six feet, four inches tall. He said to me as a little kid, "Hey, son, how would you like to go to Sunday School?" Well, anything that had "school" in it had to be bad news.

Then he said, "How would you like to play marbles?"

That was different! Would you believe we got down and played marbles, and he beat me in every single game? I lost my marbles early in life! By the time Walt got through, I didn't care where he was going— that's where I wanted to go.

For your information, he picked up 13 of us boys, nine from broken homes. Today, 11 are in full-time vocational work. And Walt never went to school beyond the sixth grade.

That's the power of a mentor. You don't need a Ph.D. to be used by God in the ministry of mentoring.[6]

Summary

Our world is rapidly changing, but the impact of mentoring has been validated throughout the centuries. Christians should have their Bibles opened on one knee and the newspaper opened on the other knee asking the question, "How does God's Word apply to our day?"

We need more "men of Issachar, who understood the times and knew what Israel should do" (2 Chron. 12:32a). May God help us to empower the next generation with biblical convictions, moral character and life skills through mentoring.

CHAPTER ONE REVIEW

DISCUSSING ISSUES

1. How is technological advancement impacting relationships in our society?

   People make less friends because some they have become computer zombies. Unschooled in communication & would rather relate to a iphone.

2. How would you define masculinity? How would you define femininity? What evidence do we see in our culture today that there is gender confusion?

   Man is purpose driven who needs to be cheered on
   Woman - nourishes & promotes friendships in relationships w/ others, needs to feel security

3. In what ways do you think mentoring can be a powerful tool in our churches, workplaces and communities today?

   Everyone needs to have someone who shows the way to the Lord. Connecting in love, honor & cherishing their conduct.

4. How can mentoring unify the varied generations in your church?

   Character training is essential to help members grow w/ Christ like role model.

STUDYING GOD'S WORD

5. Read Ephesians 5:15-17. What are ways a Christian man can "make the most of his time" in our present world?

   Keep standards high, seek Gods will, be careful

6. What is it about God's nature that shows why mentoring relationships are so important? (Consider the "Introduction" of this book focusing on Genesis 1:27 and 2:18.)

    mankind need each other.

7. Why is the biblical practice of mentoring an important model for our day as well (consider 1 Corinthians 11:1)?

    follow my example as I follow Jesus.

APPLYING GOD'S WORD

8. In what practical ways can you come alongside to mentor the young man or woman who is living a distance from his or her extended family or whose parents are divided by divorce?

    Hospitality, showing understanding, sympathy & encouragement.

9. How is your church presently developing future leaders? How could you strengthen that process through mentoring?

    Mentor by inclusiveness & presenting the sum of its parts, Together w/ Christ work is light & breezy.

10. Think about the example of from Dr. Pedrone's life. Who has made that kind of difference in your life? What did they do? How did they do it? Why did they do it?

    Bible study leaders,

KEY VERSE:

Meditate and memorize the following— Be "men of Issachar, who understood the times and knew what Israel should do . . ." (1 Chron. 12:32a).

Understanding & Knowledge

CHAPTER TWO

The Meaning of Mentoring

Various terms are used in describing the mentoring process. These words include mentor, mentoring, discipleship, empowerment, generativity, bonding, and protégé. Understanding each term will aid in discovering the meaning of mentoring.

Mentor

The word "mentor" has its origins in Greek mythology. Homer, in *The Odyssey*, describes how Odysseus appointed a guardian for his son Telemachus while he was at war. The mythical guardian's name was Mentor. The fatherly Mentor gave Telemachus advice, instruction, care, and protection.[7]

It was customary in Greece for young male citizens to be paired with older males in the hope that each boy would learn and emulate the values of his mentor, usually a friend of the boy's father or a relative. The Greeks based these relationships on a basic principle of human survival: humans learn skills, culture, and values directly from other humans whom they look up to or admire.[8]

> **Biblical discipleship through mentoring focuses not only on the person's spiritual development but more broadly on the development of the whole person in relationship to Christ.**

The role of a mentor continued to be practiced in the generational transfer of skills such as crafts. A young boy was apprenticed to a master craftsman who excelled in his trade. The young boy progressed from novice to journeyman to master under the watchful eye and exemplary workmanship of the master craftsman. A young woman learned the skills for life through the example of an experienced woman.

In the old university system a student would learn in the home of the scholar. Jonathan and Sarah Edwards, in eighteenth century New England, hosted ministers-in-training in their home. These young men would observe first-hand the rigors of pastoral ministry as well as the dynamics of marriage and personal spiritual life.

This valuable process of training significantly diminished with the onset of the employer/employee relationship in modern, industrial society. Much of the contemporary, group educational process has also lost the vital relational link of mentor and protégé.

A mentor is one who is trusted by the less experienced. The mentor is willing to listen to the protégé's needs and aspirations as well as to talk to him or her about life's experiences. The mentor's goal is to empower the protégé to become all that God has gifted the person to be both in a biblical worldview, character and practical skills.

Mentoring

Mentoring is a coaching process involving "challenging protégés to their best, supporting them when they falter, casting light on the territory ahead."[9] Bobb Biehl defines mentoring as "a relationship with someone you like, enjoy, believe in, and want to see win in life."[10]

Mentoring is an agreed-upon exchange between two individuals, a more experienced person and less experienced person, developing the less experienced person to his or her maximum potential in Christ and empowering them with abilities to meet a need, to achieve a goal, or to grow through a situation.[11] The mentor who assisted me (Peter) through my doctoral project on mentoring, Richard Tyre, summarizes it this way: *Mentoring is a brain to pick, a shoulder to cry on, and a kick in the pants.*

Howard Hendricks observes that although mentoring includes modeling, it goes beyond it in several key respects. First, modeling can take place at a distance, whereas mentoring necessitates personal involvement. A model may be relatively unknown to the person impacted. Mentoring involves bonding in a deeply personal relationship. Second, a model may be someone from the historical past, whereas a mentor must be a contemporary. And third, a person may model one aspect of character, whereas a mentoring relationship is more holistic.[12]

emphasing the importance of the whole and the interdependence of it parts = tx's

Discipleship

Mentoring has more recently been contrasted with discipleship. Some define discipleship as teaching a certain body of knowledge, primarily the spiritual disciplines. Mentoring, in contrast, has a whole life application where the mentor has a longer-lasting relationship with the protégé and stays on the protégé's agenda.

give and take

Although not all mentoring is discipleship with its emphasis on spiritual development, I believe effective discipleship *should involve mentoring*. A disciple is a learner. To become a disciple is a life objective. Mentoring is a tool, a relational process, for achieving the goal of discipleship. Discipleship through mentoring involves a dynamic interchange between the teacher and the learner. There is both mentor initiated guidance and protégé initiated learning.

Discipleship of a young person *should help him integrate his whole life around the centrality of Christ*. How does Jesus relate to his or her thought life? How does the Lord change relationships at home? How does Christianity shape involvement with other believers? How does a walk with Christ influence activities in the workplace and guide a career? Biblical discipleship through mentoring *focuses not only on the person's spiritual development but more broadly on the development of the whole person in relationship to Christ.*

Empowerment

"Nothing grows anywhere in God's universe apart from a source of strength and nutrition. The Bible frequently pictures growth by using plants. Think about how plants grow. They must be connected to something outside themselves."[13] Similarly, because people are relational in their created nature, they cannot grow and thrive apart from relationship—with God and with fellow human beings. Henry Cloud, a Christian psychologist, concludes, "We are literally to draw from the love of God and others to fuel our transformation and fruit bearing."[14]

Paul Stanley and Bobby Clinton describe mentoring as "a relational experience in which one person empowers another by sharing God-given resources."[15] *Empowerment is the personal growth that takes place through mentoring by enabling the protégé to address a need, achieve an aspiration, or develop through a situation.*

Generativity

Howard Hendricks presents this challenge: "The most compelling question every Christian person must ask is this: What am I doing today that will guarantee my impact for Jesus Christ in the next generation?" There is a need in the Church for transferring spiritual insights from one generation to the next, providing guidance to the next generation. Something significant is lost when we do not share multigenerational experiences and relationships.

Although generativity is epitomized in parenting it is also expressed in other activities such as mentoring. Mentoring is described as the process of opening our lives to others, of sharing our lives with others. It is a process of living for the next generation. *Generativity is defined as the concern for establishing and guiding the next generation.*

Bonding

A foundational building block of the mentoring relationship is trust. Trust is the degree of confidence you feel when you think about a relationship."[16] In this context, bonding is *a close relationship of trust between the mentor and protégé.* That trust must be established during the initial period of the relationship for genuine mentoring to take place. Ron Lee Davis simply defines a mentor as a "trusted counselor."[17]

Protégé

The term protégé comes from the French verb, *proteger*, which means "to protect." In the original Greek model, Mentor served as a protector of Odysseus' son Telemarkos. One of the functions of mentoring is *to provide protection for the less experienced person from obstacles that would hinder personal or career development.*

This protection involves confidentiality, concern, and guidance. Protection is provided most effectively in a context of trust. Bobb Biehl concludes: "I see mentoring as the critical link in developing, protecting, and optimizing Christian leaders for the next generation."[18]

Summary

A *protégé* is one who is willing to (1) enter into a personal relationship of trust with a *mentor* and (2) be *empowered* by that relationship. The person sharing is called a *mentor*. The person being *empowered* is called the *protégé*. There is mutuality in growth through the relationship.

The *mentoring* relationship begins with a *bond* of trust. *Mentoring* is a significant means in the process of making *disciples*. Through mentoring a mature person can impact the next *generation* for Jesus Christ.

CHAPTER TWO REVIEW

DISCUSSING ISSUES

1. Define the meaning of "mentor" in your own words.

   a teacher who focuses on building a relationship w/ Christ to further the spiritual, body + mind in wholesomeness & instruction in godly living.

2. Illustrate from your own life and experience Richard Tyre's definition of mentoring as

   "Don't be a wiener"

   "a brain to pick, *asking questions, receiving sympathy, walk your walk*
   a shoulder to cry on, and
   a kick in the pants."

   we all face life difficult times, walk in truth + love.

3. What are some examples of training that include a mentoring process?

   Discipleship classes - Bible study. Learning to serve the elderly while receiving a bounty from life's challenging experiences shared.

4. How is training through mentoring different from traditional classroom instruction?

   maturity in Christ to pass on to family + friends,

5. How does a mentor protect the less experienced person?

   nurturing their growth by using the fruit of the Spirit and trusting that God will have control, by bearing their burdens, his burden is light once you put on the yoke. not pulling alone.

STUDYING GOD'S WORD

6. How would you compare discipleship and mentoring? Are they the same? Are there differences? (Consider Mark 1:16-18).

   Discipleship - learning of Jesus mentoring - next step - taking Jesus into the core of your being + walking, talking + showing Jesus to others.

7. As you think about the Bible, who are some Old Testament examples of mentors and protégés?

MENTOR	PROTÉGÉ
Hannah	Samuel
Naomi	Ruth
Haman	Esther
	His followers
Jesus	others
mary magdalten.	humility -true faith -me
Job	

8. Who are some New Testament examples of mentors and protégés?

MENTOR	PROTÉGÉ
Jesus	Disciples (His followers)
John	
All the mary's	
matthew	
paul *	
mark	
Luke	

APPLYING GOD'S WORD

9. Define generativity. How are you investing your life in the next generation?

Showing, thru my life how to be a good wife
Showing, to my grandchildren God's love.
" sister + other relatives God's redemption
Sharing life's difficulties and process
of overcoming thru faith in Christ.

KEY VERSES:

Memorize and meditate on Psalm 1:1-2.

Stay away from wicked, sinners + mockers
meditate on God's word.

CHAPTER THREE

The Basics of Mentoring

Sit down. We are going to watch the fight!

These were the words of Dr. Paul Griffis. Uncle Paul, as he was affectionately called by many, was a professor at what was then the Practical Bible Training School, Johnson City, New York. He had invited me (Dino) to join his son Vince at his house. I had the deepest respect for him. He was tall, kind, and a deep thinker. He never told me he was my mentor nor did I ask him to mentor me but he was just that. Upon arriving at his house I was nervous. I wanted so much to fit into this scholar's home. I was not ready for "Sit down. We are going to watch the fight." Uncle Paul was a big Floyd Patterson fan. I too liked Patterson. Floyd was boxing Jimmy Ellis. When the decision was rendered, Ellis won. Uncle Paul, this mild manner scholar was livid. "Patterson won!" I agreed. At that moment I saw a glimpse into a man who was real. I liked boxing. He liked boxing. For years I found myself desiring to please this man of God. Vince, Jerry Traister (the president of our class) were often inseparable. The glue was our mentor, Dr. Paul. I remember so many times sitting and chatting in his office, living room, den, or over a cold relaxing drink. He would often ask me about what was happening in my life. On several occasions he dropped notes to me and each one of them was encouraging.

There were many lessons from this man of God but the one that stuck out in my life was this. He never told me about what I should do. When I had a question he led me in a path of questions that I myself would answer. He helped me to learn this. A mentor does not need to tell the protégé what to do but he needs to guide the conversation into a direction that would best answer the prevailing questions. He instructed by example, presence, and by a series of questions and answers. Mentoring is relational. There was something about him that made me want to be around him and especially please him. His questions were thought provoking and they helped me to understand how to travel the road I was on.

I (Peter) was introduced to the formal study of mentoring through what is now called Bethel Seminary of the East. When I was pastoring on Long Island, a promising young man in the church, Rob Sundholm, was approaching the conclusion of his college studies. He was preparing for pastoral ministry and was considering seminary options.

Bethel Seminary of the East was founded on a philosophy of education that would not only focus on theological training but also on character development and ministry skills. As a basic building block of the program, the student would enter into a mentoring relationship with both a pastor and a lay leader from his church.

Together with John Floresta, a leader in my church, I had the privilege of serving as one of Rob's mentors. We met weekly with the protégé and monthly with a support group for mentors. This relationship became a significant ministry experience for me. It was a highlight of my pastoral life. I am encouraged that more than twenty-five years later Rev. Sundholm continues to effectively serve as the pastor of Grace Baptist Church in Brooklyn, New York.

Because of this positive experience I began a formal study of mentoring. I wanted to apply the Bethel Seminary of the East's model of training to the local church setting for the purpose of developing lay leadership. First Baptist Church of Clayton, New Jersey, provided the opportunity to apply mentoring to lay leadership development. The ministry was called the Leadership Acquisition Mentoring Program (LAMP).

The commitment to mentor future leaders in the church has continued to be a priority in my current pastoral role at Faith Baptist Church. Four seminarians recently completed three years of leadership development in partnership with a nearby extension site of MidAmerica Baptist Theological Seminary. This partnership included academic and theological training primarily accomplished at the seminary. Our local church contribution focused on character development and ministry skills. The training culminated in two of the students being ordained to the Gospel ministry.

Mutual Trust

Through these mentoring relationships, we have observed several foundational principles. The first and most important element of an effective mentoring relationship is mutual trust. I (Peter) asked the participants in the mentoring program to answer this question: "What one thing is most important in establishing a relationship between a mentor and a protégé?" More than 80% of the participants identified "trust" as the most important ingredient. One mentor summarized it this way, "If the mentor and protégé are not able to feel trust for one another, the relationship will not be effective."

Trust should be established within the first few months of a mentoring relationship. Without confidence in the mentor, the protégé will not be responsive to his guidance.

Reciprocally, the mentor needs to believe in his protégé's potential. Without confidence in the protégé, the mentor would be reticent to invest time and energy in helping the younger person achieve dreams and plans. The ideal mentor looks at the protégé and says, "You have tremendous potential. I want to invest my life in you because I believe you have what it takes to make a real difference."

Basics of Mentoring
- **Mutual Trust**
- **Mutual Commitment**
- **Voluntary Participation**
- **Vulnerability**
- **Honesty**
- **Modeling**
- **Teachability**
- **Accountability**

Mutual Commitment

A second foundational principle for effective mentoring is mutual commitment. Mentoring needs the commitment of the protégé to the mentor. If you sincerely desire to learn and to grow from the wisdom of a more experienced person, you are a potential protégé. It is popularly believed that mentors choose protégés. However, no one can be mentored who does not choose to be mentored. In most cases, protégés actually choose mentors. Mentoring is often "protégé driven."[19]

Mentoring demands a reciprocal commitment of the mentor to the protégé. An effective mentor has something to share and is willing to do so. A mentor is willing to invest time and energy in the life of the less experienced person.[20]

Voluntary Participation

Third, because mentoring requires commitment, it is important that even a facilitated mentoring program has voluntary participation by both the mentors and the protégés. You cannot force the intensive personal involvement of mentoring.

In a study of the successful Merrill Lynch mentoring program, the first observation was that "one must ensure the voluntary participation of mentors."[21] This principle was also confirmed in my lay leadership mentoring program (LAMP). The LAMP was not effective when the mentor, who in that case was a church elder, was reluctant to participate in the program. Both the mentor and the protégé must have a willingness and enthusiasm to participate in the relationship.

Vulnerability

Fourth, mentoring requires vulnerability. Protégés "need to see us go through the whole gamut of life's experiences and emotions lived out before their very eyes, but in a godly way." For example, "they need to see us saddened, but never giving up hope . . . they need to see us angry at an unfair decision, but under control."[22]

Bill Lawrence observes that "vulnerability" is a "willingness to share your pilgrimage with Christ. . . when the listener is prepared to hear." The protégé looks at his own personal weaknesses when the mentor becomes vulnerable in his areas of frailty. Bill concludes, "We cannot mentor without vulnerability." He identifies vulnerability as "the primary ingredient" and "the greatest obstacle" in mentoring.[23]

Honesty

Fifth, related to vulnerability is honesty. Mentoring requires loving honesty. The Apostle Paul challenges us: "Speaking the truth in love, we will in all things grow up into him who is the Head, that is, Christ" (Eph. 4:15). And King Solomon wisely counsels us, "Wounds from a friend can be trusted" (Prov. 27:6).

Both of us have ministry colleagues who have been honest in admonishing us. They have graciously addressed faults in my life and work. What makes us appreciate the "wounds" is that these colleagues are great encouragers. We are grateful for friends who as co-mentors care enough to confront. (Co-mentors are studied in more detail in Chapter 12.)

Modeling

Sixth, the mentoring relationship entails modeling. The Apostle Paul extended an invitation, "Follow my example as I follow the example of Christ" (1 Cor. 11:1). The protégé must feel that his mentor is, in many respects, the quality of person he would like to be someday. He needs to admire and respect his mentor.

For example, in an effective youth ministry, personal modeling is crucial. Parents and church leaders should ask, "Is the youth worker what I would like my children or my students to become?"[24] A mentor to young people must "show and tell."

Teachability

A seventh quality of an effective mentoring relationship is openness to learn. Both mentor and protégé must be teachable. The purpose for entering a mentoring relationship is to grow through that relationship. Ultimately, the goal of that growth is Christlikeness. That is because God has "predestined [us] to be conformed to the likeness of his Son" (Rom. 8:29).

When the mentor is teachable, he or she models the willingness to learn. The protégé must also have that quality. We are all "in process." God is not finished with us yet. We must ask, "What can I learn from this relationship to become all God wants me to be?"

Accountability

An eighth principle, crucial to the effectiveness of a mentoring relationship is accountability. This does not mean the mentor controls the protégé. There is mutual accountability. In fact, the protégé must share his or her dreams and goals to shape the course of the mentoring relationship.

However, mentors cannot be afraid to confront. Mentors are responsible to help protégés achieve their agendas—holding them to their stated plans and helping them to assess the reasonableness of their goals. Mentors must guide and direct at teachable moments in the protégés' lives.

In the mentoring program of Bethel Seminary of the East and in my (Peter's) lay leadership development program, "learning agreements" (i.e. guided learning experiences) provided a structure for that accountability. These agreements can be adapted to an informal mentoring relationship.

I have called these accountability tools "target learning agreements" (see chapter 15 for further explanation and some examples). The objectives are targets or goals. These targets involve learning something new in thought, character, or skill. The learning tasks to achieve these targets should be reasonable and measurable. The mentor agrees to help the protégé aim for each target. Therefore, it is helpful to write down the agreement to ensure mutual understanding.

Mentoring Described

One of the clearest biblical passages describing mentoring is found in Titus 2:3-5. Paul's instruction to older women provides guidance for effective mentoring. The passage describes the mentor as a model to follow and as one who presents a message to learn. The Apostle Paul wrote:

> Likewise, teach the older women to be reverent in the way they live, not to be slanderers or addicted to much wine, but to teach what is good. Then they can train the younger women to love their husbands and children, to be self-controlled and pure, to be busy at home, to be kind, and to be subject to their husbands, so that no one will malign the word of God.

The Mentor Models

The character of the mentor is crucial to effectiveness. Before giving attention to what the mentor is to communicate, the Apostle Paul focused on the character of the mentor. The "older women" were mature. They had wisdom based on reverence for God, on lessons learned from others and on their own experiences in life.

Paul instructed the older women to be "reverent" (*hieroprepeis*) in their behavior and attitude. The word translated "reverent" is related to the word for temple worship. The demeanor of the women should reflect what would be fitting for temple service. That is, a mentor must engage in behavior that recognizes and reflects the holy presence of God.

The Apostle also instructed the mature women not to be "slanderers" (*diabolous*). That is, they should not "accuse or bring charges with hostile intent."[25] Control of the tongue is crucial for a credible mentor. The intimacy of the mentoring relationship requires confidentiality.

Paul goes on to instruct the mentor to avoid "addiction to much wine." Literally, she was not to be enslaved to the mastery of wine. Effective mentors must avoid addictions. That is certainly true of men who seek to be mentors today. Substance abuse, pornography and sexual addictions, sports obsession, television preoccupation, "workaholism", food excesses and even computer "webaholism" all detract from the competence of the mentor. It saddens us to see a couple in a restaurant not even looking at each other, but rather they are engrossed in their smart phones.

A mentor must model self-control, submission to the Word of God, and yielding to the Holy Spirit. According to Ephesians 5:18, "Do not get drunk with wine, which leads to debauchery. Instead, *be filled with* the Spirit." The effective mentor is yielded (passive tense) continually (present tense) to the filling (meaning control) of the Spirit of God.

Providing a godly example is fundamental to biblical mentoring. Mentoring requires modeling. The exemplary character of the mentor helps build the protégé's trust in him or her. Consistency between the walk and talk of the mentor provides the integrity necessary for the protégé to respect and respond to his or her guidance.

The Mentor's Message

The effective mentor teaches "what is good." This is practical advice, training in good judgment, and advice for improving life. This instruction goes beyond informing the mind to admonishing the will.

Paul explained what it means to "teach what is good." The mentor is concerned that the protégé develop Christlike attitudes, godly relationships in the home, and skills for living in society. Mentoring concerns the development of the whole person. The mentor's focus is multi-dimensional rather than narrowly concentrating only on one dimension of the protégé's life.

The mentor's passion is to help the less experienced person grow in Christlikeness. What does it mean to be "Christlike"? The Lord Jesus "grew in wisdom and stature, and in favor with God and men" (Luke 2:52). Jesus matured intellectually, physically, spiritually and socially. These areas represent the breadth of personal growth targets for the mentoring relationship.

don't mix mentoring between sexes

Women Mentoring Women and Men Mentoring Men

Another principle about mentoring from Titus 2 concerns same gender mentoring. Older women were instructed to mentor younger women. Vickie Kraft, author of *Women Mentoring Women,* supports this conclusion for the following reason: "Women can encourage women in this complex and confused society. . . [because] women understand women. Who but another woman can fully understand?"[26]

The corresponding wisdom is that men should mentor men. Bill Bright of Campus Crusade for Christ counseled Bobb Biehl, "I would advise against a man ever mentoring a young woman." This is because men best relate to and respond to male modeling. Biehl adds, "Like other helping relationships, mentoring relationships get deep enough, fast enough that the love individuals give and receive can easily be reinterpreted into sexual dimensions."[27]

Summary

A mentor must be the kind of person the protégé aspires to become. The mentor's message concerns the whole spectrum of life's experiences—conviction, character and skill. A mentoring relationship has eight key ingredients: mutual trust, mutual commitment, voluntary participation, vulnerability, honesty, modeling, teachability, and accountability.

CHAPTER THREE REVIEW

DISCUSSING ISSUES

1. If your mentor had just 6 of the 8 qualities—which two, if missing, would have the greatest impact on your relationship? Which two would have the least impact?

   greatest missing - honesty
   mutual commitment
   least needed - accountability
   vulnerability
   } really all needed

2. If your protégé had just 6 of the 8 qualities—which two, if missing, would have the greatest impact on your relationship? Which two would have the least impact?

   Same

3. What are some of the difficulties and risks associated with cross-gender mentoring?

   wrong ideas toward sexuality
   lack of trust on partner's side

STUDYING GOD'S WORD

4. What are the key principles of mentoring presented in Titus 2:3-5? Adapt these principles to your life. Which principles do you need to apply to your own life?

   Principles: busy @ home, no slander, train young
   wives to love children & husbands, be kind, subjective,

APPLYING GOD'S WORD

5. Consider Luke 2:52 and Romans 8:29. How is Christ's life demonstrated in the following areas of your life: intellectually, physically, spiritually and socially?

   Intellectually - for exalted knowledge of rabbis, but became
   obedient to parents & trusted
   physically - exercise, eat, do not be idol
   spiritually - seek the word, obey the laws, meditate (pray)
   Socially - treat others carefully, kindness + preference

   Luke: after being obedient to parents he grew Trust
   Rom: predestined to be conformed to the likeness of his son

6.   Reflect on a potential mentor or protégé for a mentoring relationship. Consider below the name of a potential mentor or a potential protégé. Do you feel he has the qualities of a mentor or protégé? If the quality is generally true of that person, place a check next to the corresponding quality.

MENTOR:	QUALITY	PROTÉGÉ:
	Mutual Trust	
	Commitment	
	Voluntary	
	Vulnerability	
	Honesty	
✓	*Modeling*	
✓	*Teachability*	
	Accountability	

7.   Now circle the mentoring qualities listed above that you want to focus on for development in your own life.

Voluntary
Vulnerability
modeling
accountability
commitment

KEY VERSE:

Meditate on and memorize Ephesians 5:18.

Do not get drunk on wine which leads to debauchery. Instead be filled with the Spirit.

Bonding describes the "mystery of human attachment between two persons."[28] There are various kinds of bonding. The first kind of bonding takes place in the mother-child relationship called "birth bonding."[29] A second kind of bonding results in a romantic relationship between a man and a woman.[30] A third kind is the "kindred spirit" between close friends. Our study focuses on a fourth kind of bonding—that of a mentor and a protégé.

Bonding Defined

Bonding in mentoring is a close relationship of trust between the mentor and protégé. It is established during the initiation phase—the first 3-6 months—of an effective mentoring relationship. This initiation phase allows the participants to determine if they want to continue. A relationship is coaching or advising, but not true mentoring until bonding takes place.

Bonding Developed

What factors help develop a bond of trust in a mentoring relationship? The first factor is the mentor's *competence*. You have confidence in a mentor who is skilled in life and work. Although technical competence is important in engendering trust, the mentor's interpersonal skills are of greater significance. Does your mentor listen? Does he or she care about your interests or only his or her own agenda? Does the mentor model his or her message?[31]

Second, developing a bond of trust takes *time together*. Time together requires availability and accessibility. Because of the scarcity of our time, we should consider developing mentoring relationships with those potential mentors who already have regular contact points in our lives. We can infuse purpose into our casual relationships by developing mentoring relationships.[32]

Factors in Bonding
- **Competent Mentor**
- **Time Together**
- **Symbiosis**
- **Common Problem**
- **Open-Mindedness/ Active Listening**
- **Self-disclosure**
- **Genuine Care**

—shared background & interests

A third factor necessary to bonding is *symbiosis*. Symbiosis involves sharing something in common. As Christians we share our commitment to Jesus Christ. Symbiosis may be enhanced by a shared theological or denominational perspective. Symbiosis is strengthened by:

(1)   shared backgrounds—you both grew up on a farm;
(2)   shared interests—you both love NFL football or serving at the city mission;

(3)   shared hobbies—you can't wait for deer season or you both enjoy knitting;

(4)   common vocations—you are ministry buddies, are moms or dads, or you both are plumbers or teachers; *Linda Suttridge*

(5)   shared educational pursuits—you are both finishing your MBA; and

(6)   geographical proximity—you live in the same town.

All of these common experiences help bonding to take place.[33] Who do you know who shares some of your values and interests? This person is a potential mentor or protégé. *Anne Mary, Sarah, Joan Henry,*

A fourth key for developing bonding is that the mentor and protégé face a *common problem*.[34] Men bond more readily when they work together to paint a wall, to solve a problem, to compete on a team against an athletic opponent, or to climb a mountain. Bonding is energized when two people work together to overcome obstacles to reach a common goal. Women enjoy time together, sharing life's relationships.

Fifth, bonding involves *open-mindedness* and *active listening*. Bonding is built upon the understanding that the mentor and protégé do not need to agree on every issue. When there is bonding, the participants appreciate their differences. Because they respect one another, they listen to each other's perspectives.

A sixth factor found important to engender a bond of trust in a mentoring relationship is *self-disclosure*. This means sharing what is happening on the inside. It is timely disclosure of your personal failures and disappointments as well as successes.[35] William Stewart asks, "Why is it that so few great men of God raise up great men of God?" His observation was this: "In fact, some of us are not inclined to allow another the closeness and trust required for an authentic mentor relationship."[36]

Finally, *genuine care* for one another is the subtle, the most important, and perhaps the most rare of all the elements in bonding. A true mentor is a friend who sticks closer than a brother. Genuine love goes the extra mile. Mentoring is described as "a powerful, *emotional interaction* between an older and younger person, a relationship in which the older member is trusted and experienced in the guidance of the younger. The mentor helps shape the development of the protégé (*italics mine*)."[37]

Bonding Demonstrated

The biblical account of Ruth's life demonstrates the importance of bonding in mentoring. She sought the help and guidance of a more experienced person in the faith. Ruth, whose name may mean "friendship," initiated a mentoring relationship with her mother-in-law Naomi. They lived during the turbulent biblical times of the judges. They showed faithfulness among a faithless people.

At the center of Ruth's love and commitment to her mentor was a deep respect for Naomi and a commitment to know her God.[38] Naomi was a competent mentor. She taught Ruth about God's "faithfulness" (*hesed*) toward his people. After they both endured the common problem of widowhood, "Naomi said to her daughters-in-law, 'Go back, each of you, to your mother's home. May the Lord show kindness [*hesed*] to you, as you have shown to your dead and to me'" (Ruth 1:8). It is the Hebrew word, *hesed*, which points us to faithfulness as the Book of Ruth's main theme (see 2:20; 3:10). *Hesed* means loving-kindness, loyalty, compassion (see Micah 6:8)."[39] Ruth's relationship with Naomi was rooted in a shared dependence upon the Lord.

Instead of leaving, "Ruth clung [*dabaq*] to Naomi" (Ruth 1:14b). The Hebrew verb *dabaq* means committed, faithful "cleaving" in a deep personal connection. The word was used of Adam's relationship with his wife in the Garden.[40] "For this reason a man will leave his father and mother and be united to (*dabaq*) his wife, and they will become one flesh" (Gen. 2:24). The meaning of *dabaq* parallels that of bonding— a close relationship of trust.

Ruth was deeply bonded to Naomi as revealed in Ruth 1:16-17.

But Ruth replied, "Don't urge me to leave you or to turn back from you. Where you go I will go, and where you stay I will stay. Your people will be my people and your God will be my God. Where you die I will die, and there I will be buried. May the Lord deal with me, be it ever so severely, if anything but death separates you and me."

Ruth probably had Semitic burial customs in mind here. Normally, Semites bury their dead family members in a common grave. Ruth promised that she would die in Israel and be buried there with Naomi's family. This shut the door on any future return to her homeland of Moab. Here Ruth modeled a commitment that is total and final.[41] "This classic expression of loyalty and love discloses the true character of Ruth. Her commitment to Naomi is complete, even though it offers no prospect for her except to share in Naomi's desolation."[42]

Ruth, a protégé, was determined to spend time with her mentor. Ruth's interest and commitment was the catalyst in making Naomi an effective mentor. Ruth's relationship with Naomi exemplifies a protégé-driven mentoring relationship. The protégé trusted both her mentor and her mentor's Lord.

Ruth's bond with Naomi enabled this dedicated learner to receive her mentor's guidance. Bonding was the glue of this mentoring relationship. They listened to and shared with one another. Naomi recommended, "It will be good for you, my daughter to go with his girls, because in someone else's field you might be harmed" (Ruth 2:22). Naomi's counsel meant two things. First, she wanted Ruth to accept Boaz' offer by working only in his field. Second, Naomi steered Ruth away from the male workers toward the female ones. Naomi deeply cared for her protégé's wellbeing. Naomi's aim was to divert Ruth from potential romances with workers until her relationship with Boaz could run its course. Perhaps she also wanted to guard Ruth's chastity.[43]

Naomi later counseled Ruth concerning her relationship with Boaz (Ruth 3:1-5). Naomi helped him to become a "kinsman-redeemer" (*go'el*). This ancient practice involved marrying the widow of a relative and buying his property. This was a selfless act in that the children born of this relationship received the name of the deceased. They also inherited the land. In this way the people of Israel preserved the family line and property of the man who died.

Summary

Bonding, a close relationship of trust, is the crucial first phase of a mentoring relationship. Bonding is developed through the mentor's competence, time together with the protégé, symbiosis, facing a common problem, active listening, self-disclosure and genuine care. Ruth's relationship with Naomi illustrated each of the ingredients that help develop bonding.

Ruth and Naomi's connection also demonstrated three important principles in mentoring. First, a committed bond of trust is the glue for an effective mentoring relationship. Second, mentoring is often "protégé-driven." And third, Naomi exercised the true role of a mentor who "protected" the younger, less experienced protégé from potential hazards that could hinder her from achieving the fullest potential.

CHAPTER FOUR REVIEW

DISCUSSING ISSUES

1. Define "bonding" in your own words.

A relationship grow together thru loving kindness, caring or kindred spirit Tuning to God & not overwhelming one another w/ea. others giving, but understanding of another

need for Christ to bear our burdens

2. Review and define the components that facilitate bonding. From your own relationship with others illustrate each of these components.

   a. Mentor's **common** *interests & outlook on life*

   b. **Spending time given together** together *(listening & waiting eyes the Lord.*

   c. Sharing something in *mind, body & Spirit*

   d. Face a common *goal & interests*

   e. Open-minded and active *relationship that promotes openess & healing*

   f. Self- *discovery thru another's eyes, critical but tenderly honest*

   g. Genuine *Care, love & kindness* for one another

STUDYING GOD'S WORD

3. Who initiated the mentoring relationship between Naomi and Ruth? Do you feel that mentoring relationships are mentor-initiated, protégé-driven, or both?

   Ruth initiated. Work both ways, clearly & open ended call by both mentor & protégé

4. Identify the seven components that facilitate bonding as they appear in Ruth's relationship with Naomi. For example, they faced a common problem in that they both were widowed.

   1. background
   2. interests
   3. ideas
   4. vocation
   5. pursuits
   6. geographic proximity
   7. Holy Spirit driven

5. Why was the mentoring relationship between Naomi and Ruth so effective? Compare the use of the word "cleave" or "united to" in Ruth 1:14 and Genesis 2:24. Applying God's Word

Ruth 1:14 separation between daughter in laws
Ruth clung - didn't want to leave her
Gen 2:24 leave father + mother
cleave to wife

APPLYING GOD'S WORD

6. William Stewart asks, "Why is it that so few great men of God raise up great men of God? In fact some of us are not inclined to allow another the closeness and trust required for an authentic mentoring relationship. What do you think about William Stewart's observation? Why don't men mentor more often? Why don't women mentor more often?

They may be dealing w/ their own walk + don't trust God enough to allow someone else to come alongside.

7. What fears and concerns do you have concerning entering into a mentoring relationship?

That once you allow someone to watch your walk closely they may reject your actions or deeds + become disillusioned. Each needs to find their own pace.

KEY VERSES:

Meditate on and memorize Ruth 1:16-17. This passage is used in wedding ceremonies but originally had more application to a mentoring relationship.

Don't urge me to leave you or turn back from you. Where you go I will go, and where you stay I will stay. Your people will be my people and your God will be my God. Where you are buried so will I. May the Lord deal severely with me, if anything but death separates you + me.

Ruth made a commitment - to death do us part.

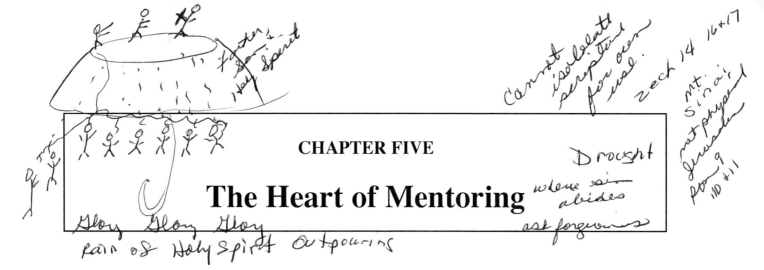

Handwritten annotations (top of page): Father's, Son's, Holy Spirit; Cannot isolate scripture for our use; Zech 14 16+17; mt. sinai not physical Jerusalem; Drought where sin abides; ask forgiveness; Glory Glory Glory; Rain of Holy Spirit Outpouring

CHAPTER FIVE

The Heart of Mentoring

Dr. James Dobson uses the analogy of a three-man relay race to illustrate the transfer of the Gospel from one generation to the next. He likens the Gospel to the baton. First, your father runs his lap around the track carrying the baton. At the appropriate moment, he hands the baton to you, and you begin your journey around the track. Then finally, the time comes when you must get the baton safely in the hands of your child.

Coaches note that relay races are usually won or lost at the passing of the baton. Rarely is the baton dropped on the far side of the track when the runner has it firmly in his grasp. There is a critical moment when all can be lost by a fumble or miscalculation. Runners may drop the baton in attempting to transfer it. If failure occurs in transferring the Gospel, it will likely happen in the exchange between generations.

> **The Church has an urgent need to transfer spiritual truth from one generation to the next.**

The Church has an urgent need to transfer spiritual truth from one generation to the next. We must provide guidance for the next generation. Although parenting is most important in this process, mentoring also helps the transfer. Mentoring is a process of living for the next generation. Generativity is the concern for guiding and establishing the next generation.

The Apostle Paul instructed Timothy concerning mentoring future leaders in 2 Timothy 2:1-2. This passage emphasizes the importance of trust in the transfer of spiritual truth and leadership skills.

> You then, my son, be strong in the grace that is in Christ Jesus. And the things you have heard me say in the presence of many witnesses entrust to reliable men who will also be qualified to teach others.

Paul's association with Timothy closely parallels the nature of mentoring. The Apostle both practiced mentoring and instructed his disciple concerning the process of mentoring. First, he served as a mentor to Timothy. Then he instructed his protégé to be a mentor to "reliable men." And finally, Paul expected that those reliable men would become mentors to others. Thus, these verses of Scripture reveal three "generations" of mentoring relationships.

Paul's mentoring of Timothy entailed trust. "You, then, my son," is an expression that shows the tender affection of a spiritual father for a spiritual son. Besides respect and honor, a fundamental dimension of a son's relationship to his father is trust.

Trust is the most important building block in the foundation of an effective mentoring commitment. It is the confidence you feel when you think about a relationship. A mentor is a trusted counselor or guide. He earns that trust by the quality and genuineness of his life.

Strength for Mentoring

Paul's counsel to Timothy began by identifying the strength for mentoring leaders. "Be strong in the grace that is in Christ Jesus" (2 Tim. 2:1). Strength for the task is found in the grace of God. Grace is God's undeserved favor. God's grace provides salvation through faith in the Lord Jesus Christ (Eph. 2:8-9). His grace also enables believers to grow in him and to serve him.

At the inception of Paul's second epistle to Timothy, he has already challenged his protégé concerning the resources for ministry: "For God did not give us a spirit of timidity, but a spirit of power, of love and of self-discipline" (2 Tim. 1:7). Timothy's strength for mentoring cannot be found within himself. A person is sure to fail when relying on human resources alone. However, God does not ask us to accomplish a task without also giving us the power to do it.

Substance of Mentoring

The Apostle continued, "and the things you have heard me say in the presence of many witnesses" (2 Tim. 2:2a). In the context of this epistle, these "things" are the truths of God's Word. These are truths both about salvation from God and about ministering for him. These "things" include both the message and the methods. The transferring of leadership skills entails teaching spiritual truths and modeling ministry.

Setting for Mentoring

Howard and William Hendricks draw a mentoring principle from the phrase "in the presence of many witnesses." The mentoring relationship itself needs "checks and balances." Paul and Timothy's relationship did not occur in secret. Accountability came from others who observed what was being said and done. The counsel of the mentor should be balanced with the viewpoints of others and certainly with the authority of the Bible.[44] This principle points to the value of not only one-on-one mentoring but also accountability relationships in small groups.

There was a young adult in my (Peter's) church on Long Island who was overly dependent on the directives of a mentor. The protégé was immobilized without the step-by-step instruction of the mentor. That young adult had abdicated personal responsibility. That mentor had usurped control and cultivated an excessive dependency.

Selection of Mentors

The Apostle Paul's plan for leadership development involved selecting capable mentors. Timothy was to mentor men who would in turn mentor others. Timothy was given the responsibility to "entrust to reliable men who will also be qualified to teach others" (2 Tim. 2:2b). Notice that the first qualification in this chain was faithfulness or trustworthiness. The second qualification was competence to teach others.[45]

The word translated "reliable" is literally "faithful" (*pistois*). This character trait describes both trusting in God and being found trustworthy.[46] These men can be counted on to complete the task. The key quality of Timothy's protégés, who in turn would become mentors, is that they be found "trustworthy." Current research echoes the biblical principle that trustworthiness is foundational to an effective mentoring relationship.

An important aspect of the biblical examples of mentoring is cultivating close relationships of trust. Protégés respond to the counsel and guidance of those in whom they have confidence. The mentor earns that trust through his character, competence and concern.

Strategy for Mentoring

How did Paul instruct Timothy to transfer spiritual truth and leadership skills to others? Paul described the strategy or process in the one word, "entrust" (*parathou*). This means "to give someone something in trust."[47] This transfer of spiritual truth and wisdom from a more experienced person to a less experienced person is the essence of the mentoring relationship.

Paul instructed Timothy to multiply ministry through others. The apostle anticipated that trained leaders "will also be qualified to teach others" (2 Tim. 2:2b). The word translated "qualified" (*hikanoi*) means ability demonstrated by repeated application.[48] These men have a proven track record because they have been involved in ministry as apprentices. One test of training effectiveness is the competence of the learner to serve in the leader's absence.

To be "qualified" speaks of competence. Competence is the ability to do the task with excellence. There is no substitute for competence in your work and excellence in your ministry. Sincerity is crucial but it is no substitute for sweat. You remember training for the track meet, practicing for the piano recital, or studying for the exam. You know how much preparation goes into being a master plumber, a persuasive lawyer, a skilled artist, or an effective teacher! You trust the doctor who has studied hard and practiced diligently. Competence yields confidence.

Summary

How are spiritual leaders to "entrust to reliable men" the spiritual truths and principles they have learned? In Scripture mentoring is regularly used for developing leaders. God used experienced leaders as mentors to empower future leaders for their divinely appointed ministries.

The *strength* for mentoring is God's grace. The *substance* of the process includes both spiritual truths and practical skills. The *setting* for mentoring should include the accountability of the wider community of believers. In the *selection* of mentors and protégés the key quality to look for is trustworthiness. The *strategic* goal of mentoring is to multiply ministry through others.

CHAPTER FIVE REVIEW

DISCUSSING ISSUES

1. Why is trust the most important building block in the foundation of a mentoring relationship?

   Trust God
   " man/woman
   " leading of the Holy Spirit

2. What ministries in your church are designed to reach the next generation for Christ? How effectively are they accomplishing that goal?

   can't judge
   womens ministries - teaching the Word
   retreats
   demonstrating their
   effective leadership

STUDYING GOD'S WORD

3. We often feel <u>inadequate</u> for the tasks God has for us to do *including mentoring*. How can the following Scriptures help us overcome this? *inadequaces*

   Joshua 1:9 *Be strong + courageous - the Lord God will be*
   with you wherever you go

   John 15:5 *connected to the vine*

   2 Corinthians 12:9 *my GRACE is sufficient for you*
   my power is made perfect in weakness

   Philippians 4:13 *I can do everything thru Him*
   who gives me strength

4. Read 2 Timothy 2:2. Define the following words:

   "Grace" *God redemptive act thru Christs Example*

   "Things" *Word of God*

   "Entrust" *take care to pass to the thirsty*

   "Reliable" *in authority + are conducive to the spread of the gospel*

   "Qualified" *well done thru the Holy Spirit*

APPLYING GOD'S WORD

5. Based on 2 Timothy 2:1-2 describe the kind of training that could develop future leaders in your church.

   Trained under the leadership of elders who walk their walk knowing from whom all God's power humbly dwells.

6. We are inclined to associate with others of our same generation. How are you investing (or could you invest) in the next generation?

   In your family. . . . *showing a loving relationship to daughter, grandchildren + showing forgiveness to husband (example)*

   In your church. . .

   In your community. . .
   Helping people w/ reservations serving on pool committee to promote fairness to all including younger generations

7. Trust is the foundation of mentoring. Are you trustworthy? That is, are you a person of char-acter, competence and concern? Which one of these areas needs work? Be specific. Ask God for a mature brother or sister in Christ to help you progress in that area of your life.

   competence - various road blocks

KEY VERSE:

Memorize and meditate on 2 Timothy 2:2.

2:1 you then my son be strong in the grace which is Christ Jesus
2:2 + the things you have heard me say, in the presence of many witnesses entrust to reliable men who will also be qualified to teach others

CHAPTER SIX

Mentors Are Encouragers

Do you have a nickname? Perhaps you had a nickname as a young person. I (Peter) overheard a teacher greet a fellow student in my middle school saying, "Hi Smiley!"

"What a great nickname," I thought. "As a Christian I should have a nickname like that." So I determined to earn the nickname "Smiley."

I smiled whenever I could . . . all the time . . . even when it was inappropriate! But no one called me "Smiley" until one day I stopped over to see my best friend, Steve Litke. His grandmother greeted me at the door, and, of course, I smiled.

She said, "What a great smile. You should be called, 'Smiley.'" I finally had earned the nickname!

I went to school the next day and happened to be introduced to "Smiley." His name was "Mark Smiley." He hadn't earned the nickname; Smiley was his surname!

The apostles gave a man named Joseph the nickname Barnabas which means "Son of Encouragement" (*huios parakleseos*, Acts 4:36). Joseph was his Hebrew name. He was from a Levitical family. He was also given an Aramaic nickname, Barnabas, which reflected his character as a "son of encouragement." The use of the expression "son of" is a description of his character as in the proverbial statement, "like father, like son."

If there is one word in the New Testament that describes mentoring it is the word encouragement. Barnabas was an effective mentor who exemplified encouragement.

Explanation of Encouragement

The Greek word translated "encouragement" (*parakleseos*) literally means "one called alongside." Have you been encouraged simply by a person's presence during a time of need?

When I (Peter) was beginning ministry as a youth pastor in Narragansett, Rhode Island, I contracted an infection that caused a high fever. I finally agreed to go to the emergency room. As I was waiting alone in a small cubicle for the E.R. physician to attend to me Don Smith, my pastor and mentor, slipped into the room. He simply put his hand on my shoulder and I began to weep. Without a word spoken, my mentor's presence was a comfort. I had wanted to give all my energy to this new ministry and instead I was physically depleted.

The word translated "encouragement" may also be translated exhortation.[49] The word means both comfort and challenge—depending on the need of the recipient. Encouragement is not flattery. It is an honest appraisal—"speaking the truth in love" (Eph. 5:15).

If you are coaching a less experienced person, he will need both encouragement and exhortation—a shoulder to cry on and a kick in the pants! Lou Holtz, the long-time head football coach for Notre Dame and then South Carolina, understood this principle in his coaching style. He said, "You praise loudly and criticize softly."

My mother is an encourager who applies this principle, "Catch them doing something right." Focus on the positives. Don't focus on failures. Find and affirm accomplishments in the life of your protégé.

Enablement to be an Encourager

When explaining encouragement, the Bible identifies the resources necessary for being a encourager. I (Peter) can best illustrate those resources through an experience I had during my first year as a student at Wheaton College, Illinois. During the fall semester I descended into a valley of despair. I was away from home. I was lonely. I was overtired from playing soccer each afternoon and studying late into the evenings. I was wrestling with spiritual questions. Is God really there? Is Jesus the way to know him? Does he care about me?

Late one evening I read the play *No Exit* by the French existential atheist, Jean Paul Sartre. In the play Sartre vividly described the emptiness of life if there is no God. When I closed the book, I felt hopeless.

In desperation, I reached for my Bible and kneeled at my bed-side chair. I pleaded with God to speak to me. I let my Bible open on the seat of the chair. I placed my index finger on the open page resting on these words, "Simon, Simon . . ." That is Simon *Peter*. *My* name is Peter. The Lord was speaking to me!

The Word of God empowered by the Spirit of God speaking through a man of God brings encouragement.

"Simon, Simon, behold, Satan has demanded permission to sift you like wheat; but I have prayed for you, that your faith may not fail; and you, when once you have turned again, strengthen your brothers" (Luke 22:31-32). I felt that my life was being sifted like wheat— tossed into the air with a pitchfork. The chaff was being blown away leaving the valuable kernel of wheat to fall to the ground. That night, I sensed God's Spirit encouraging my heart through the Scriptures. The Bible gave me a ray of hope promising that the Lord Jesus was praying for me.

The following day a fellow student, Charlie Barker, came "alongside" and shared that he had also gone through a time of depression. I thought I was the only one. Just knowing someone had been there, and was now feeling better, was an encouragement. Because of this encounter with God's Word, His Spirit and a faithful friend in Christ, I am writing the words of this book to "strengthen *my* brothers." The *Word* of God (Rom. 15:4) empowered by the *Spirit* of God (Acts 9:31) spoken through a *man* of God (Acts 11:23-24) brings encouragement.

The Holy Spirit is identified by the Lord Jesus as the *parakletos* (e.g. John 14:26). He is the Comforter, the Helper, the Encourager. One evidence of the Spirit's presence and power in a Christian's life is that the believer encourages others.

Barnabas was "full of the Holy Spirit" (Acts 11:24). I understand "full" to signify control. In Ephesians 5:18 the filling of the Holy Spirit is contrasted with being drunk with, and thus controlled by, wine. When Barnabas' life was "full of the Holy Spirit," he was under the control of the Encourager and thus he encouraged others.

Examples of Encouragement

Barnabas is an example of an encourager. Encouragement was crucial to his effectiveness as a mentor. I have found five principles about encouragement from Barnabas' mentoring ministry.

Principle One: A mentor encourages by *observing* his protégé's needs and *meeting* them. #1 "Joseph, a Levite from Cyprus, whom the apostles called Barnabas (which means Son of Encouragement), sold a field he owned and brought the money and put it at the apostles' feet" (Acts 4:36-37).

Barnabas observed the needy Christians in his community. He then took a specific action to help meet that need. His encouragement was expressed in the practical terms of giving. He sold a piece of property that he owned. Similarly, the giving of our time, talent and treasure can be a means of encouraging another believer.

As a young pastor I (Peter) had one suit which was a bit worn on the edges and definitely out-of-style. My father-in-law, who was also my mentor, met me at a large department store in North Jersey. I thought we were going to spend time visiting together. Instead, he took me to the men's clothing department and suggested, "Let's try on some suits." That day, he bought me two suits — a black one for weddings and funerals, and a gray one for weekly services.

An encourager helps meet needs that will help the protégé move forward in reaching personal objectives. I would caution against giving financially as the core of a mentoring relationship. It is better to give perspective and time — and point the protégé to a network of resources.

Principle Two: A mentor encourages by looking #2 for evidence of God's *grace* at work in the protégé's life. The mentor sees the protégé's *future potential* based on God's enablement, not on past failure. "When he [Saul] came to Jerusalem, he tried to join the disciples, but they were all afraid of him, not believing that he really was a disciple. But Barnabas took him and brought him to the apostles. He told them how Saul on his journey had seen the Lord and that the Lord had spoken to him, and how in Damascus he had preached fearlessly in the name of Jesus" (Acts 9:27-28).

How would you have felt toward this persecutor of the church? Saul was present at and had approved of the execution of Stephen. The disciples in Jerusalem were afraid of Saul.

I (Peter) can empathize with their response. I was representing my church at a United World Mission conference in St. Petersburg, Florida. My flight arrived at the airport in Tampa where a man greeted me. He said he was there to give me a ride to my meetings. He was a tall, strong man with deep lines in his weathered face. I got into the car that he provided and we headed across the bridge to St. Pete.

As was my habit to start conversations, I asked my chauffeur, "Tell me a little about yourself." He replied, "I am a murderer."

I felt very uneasy! Had I gotten into the right car? Could I trust this man?

My driver went on to tell me that in a drunken rage he had struck and killed a man in a bar room brawl. He was arrested, tried, convicted, and incarcerated in a maximum-security prison in Ohio.

In that prison he was invited to a Bible study. He attended and after several months of watching and asking questions, he trusted Christ for the forgiveness of his sin. Subsequently, his life was remarkably changed.

Several years later, after repeated appeals by some Christian friends, he was pardoned by the Governor of Ohio. Through these friends he was given the opportunity to serve the Lord at the United World Mission headquarters.

I understand how the Jerusalem believers may have felt toward Saul. "They were afraid of him, not really believing he was a disciple." In contrast, Barnabas showed the heart of a mentor in his relationship with Saul. He courageously expressed trust in Saul. The Bible literally says that Barnabas "took hold of" Saul and brought him to the Apostles.

An important principle underlies Barnabas' actions. He didn't look at Saul's past failures. Instead he saw the grace of God at work in his life. He didn't trust in Saul but he trusted God's grace and power at work transforming Saul's life. Barnabas saw a man from the perspective of what God could do in and through his life. The mentor believes in his protégé's future potential.

A poet has written,

> If you wish to be disappointed, look at others;
> if you wish to be disheartened, look at yourself;
> if you wish to be encouraged, look to Jesus.
> And I would add, "And look to what Jesus can do in and through a believer's life.

Barnabas exhibited four important characteristics of a mentor on this occasion. First, as a mentor he cultivated a relationship with Paul. Second, he was willing to take a risk on this young believer because he believed in what God was doing in his protégé's life. Third, Barnabas is respected by the other believers in Jerusalem. And fourth, Barnabas provided his protégé with a network of resources.

Principle Three: A mentor encourages by *empowering* the protégé for expanded work and ministry. When the Gospel was received in the Gentile city of Antioch, the church in Jerusalem wanted to send a representative to strengthen the new believers. Who do you think they would send? Of course, "they sent Barnabas to Antioch" (Acts 11:22b).

What did Barnabas see when he arrived? He could have focused on the faults and past failures of these Gentiles because of their sordid background in false religion and immorality. Instead, when he arrived "he saw the evidence of the grace of God" (Acts 11:23a). He saw God's unmerited favor in saving, sanctifying, and strengthening the people of Antioch. An encourager does not dwell on past sins but looks to future progress and potential through God's grace and enablement (Acts 11:22-26).

What qualities in Barnabas' life made him such an encourager? "He was a good man, full of the Holy Spirit and faith. . ." (Acts 11:24). Barnabas was full of the Encourager. And his faith helped him to anticipate what God would do in the lives of these believers.

Barnabas combined encouraging these young believers with mentoring his protégé Paul. Barnabas observed the needs of the church in Antioch and recognized an opportunity for Paul's ministry. This mentor was an advocate for the Gentile believers and for Paul, the future Apostle to the Gentiles. "Barnabas went to Tarsus to look for Saul, and when he found him, brought him to Antioch. So for a whole year Barnabas and Saul met with the church and taught great numbers of people" (Acts 11:25-26). A mentor looks for opportunities to empower the protégé and to release him into expanded opportunities to use his God-given talents in ministry.

Principle Four: A mentor encourages by caring enough to confront the protégé. Paul prepared for a second missionary journey to encourage the young churches he had planted on his first trip. Who would he take with him on this important task? "Barnabas wanted to take John, also called Mark, with them, but Paul did not think it wise to take him, because he had deserted them in Pamphylia and had not continued with them in the work" (Acts 15:37-38).

John Mark traveled with Barnabas and Paul on their first missionary journey. However, only half way into the trip, John Mark quit and returned to Jerusalem (Acts 13:13). Why did he bail out? Perhaps he was weary of the travels because of the rugged, mosquito infested mountains of Asia Minor. Perhaps he was fearful of the persecution and resistance to the preaching of the Gospel. Perhaps he was simply homesick.

Paul and Barnabas had a "sharp disagreement" about whether or not they should take John Mark with them (Acts 15:39). Barnabas felt deeply about what Paul was doing and he cared enough to confront his protégé. Who was right? Was Barnabas right in wanting to give John Mark another chance or was Paul right in excluding him? Was John Mark going to hinder the effectiveness of the mission? Perhaps he wasn't ready for the rigors of the ministry?

Of course, Paul was right. He was the Apostle. The balance of the Book of Acts focuses on God's blessing in Paul's ministry. But, perhaps Barnabas was also right. His assessment of Mark's future potential was accurate. Mark later writes the Gospel of Mark under the direction of the Apostle Peter and the inspiration of the Holy Spirit. And at the conclusion of Paul's ministry he wrote to Timothy saying: "Get Mark and bring him with you because he is helpful to me" (2 Tim. 4:11). Although Mark wasn't ready now, under Barnabas' mentoring, he would be ready for significant responsibilities in the future.

Principle Five: An effective mentor encourages by propelling the protégé to excel beyond his or her own accomplishments. The ministry team that began as "Barnabas and Saul" (Acts 13:2) later became "Paul and Barnabas" (Acts 13:42). There is significance in the change in order of the names. In the beginning Barnabas was the prominent leader of the ministry. However, later Paul becomes the leader and Barnabas moves to the background as the supporter. For this reason, some view these men as co-mentors.

Expression of Encouragement

Are you an encourager? If you are going to be an effective mentor, encouragement is crucial. As I (Peter) traveled and spoke in various churches, I frequently asked, "Where is the most difficult place in the world to be an encourager?" Some look puzzled for a moment, but the answer is always the same. "Home" is the most difficult place to be an encourager. A mentor must model encouragement beginning at home.

Are you an encourager to your spouse? Katherine, the wife of Martin Luther, dramatically revived the reformer's confidence in God's providence.

An historical event in Martin Luther's life is described in poetic form by F.W. Herzberger.

> One day when skies loomed the blackest,
> This greatest and bravest of men
> Lost heart and in an over sad spirit
> Refused to take courage again,

Neither eating or drinking nor speaking
To anxious wife, children or friends,
Till Katherine dons widow garments
and deepest of mourning pretends.

Surprised, Luther asked why she sorrowed.
'Dear Doctor,' his Katie replied,
I have cause for the saddest of weeping,
For God in His heaven has died!"

Her gentle rebuke did not fail him,
He laughingly kissed his wise spouse,
Took courage, and banished his sorrow,
And joy again reigned in the house.

Are you an encouragement to your children? Former NFL football player and evangelist Bill Glass asked a group of a thousand prison inmates, "How many of you had parents who told you that you would end up in prison one day?" Almost every one of the prisoners raised his hand. They fulfilled their parents' discouraging expectations.

In contrast, we need to be a source of encouragement to the next generation. When he was a young boy, the great painter Benjamin West decided to sketch a picture of his sister while his mother was not at home. He got out a bottle of ink and started, but soon had an awful mess. His mother eventually returned and saw the disaster.

What would you have said? Benjamin's mother looked at the mess. She looked at the picture. Then, instead of scolding him, she picked up the portrait and declared, "What a beautiful picture of your sister!" Then she gave him a big kiss.

Later in life Benjamin West wrote in his autobiography: "With that kiss I became a painter." I would say, "With my mother's kiss, my dad's encouragement and the mentoring of many others, I became a pastor." Who will your children become because of your encouragement?

Are you an encourager at church? That is another "family" context where it is difficult to be an encourager.

During the Boer War at the siege of Ladysmith, the future of the town and fort were hanging in the balance. A civilian walked along the lines of soldiers and spoke discouraging words to the men on duty. He did not hurt anyone physically. Yet, he was arrested and sentenced to a year in prison. The crime was speaking disheartening words at a critical hour.

The church is in a critical hour of warfare. We are being assaulted by the "flaming arrows of the evil one" (Eph. 6:16). I once heard Ron Hutchins identify the Evil One's strategy against the church to be, "Shoot the chief!" We are hurting the spiritual point men who lead the church in pastoral and leadership roles. Be an encouragement to your pastor and the spiritual leadership team in your church.

One of the significant ways to be an encourager is through mentoring. Mentoring in the church can be done in informal relationships or in facilitated programs. Maximize your relationships in the church. "And let us consider how we may spur one another on toward love and good deeds. Let us not give up meeting together, as some are in the habit of doing, but let us encourage one another, and all the more as you see the Day approaching" (Heb.10:24-25).

Are you an encourager in your place of employment? Do you exhibit the character of the Encourager as you work with others? A significant platform for witnessing is encouragement. Look for opportunities to build up rather than to tear down. As a result of Barnabas' life of encouragement in the city of Antioch "a great number of people were brought to the Lord" (Acts 11:24).

Summary

Encouragement engenders hope. It is both comfort—a shoulder to cry on—and exhortation—a kick in the pants! The word of God empowered by the Spirit of God speaking through a man of God brings encouragement.

A mentor encourages by:

- observing the protégé's needs and meeting them;

- looking for evidence of God's grace at work in the protégé's life;

- empowering the protégé for expanded work and ministry;

- caring enough to confront the protégé; and

- propelling the protégé to excel beyond his or her own accomplishments.

An effective mentor begins by encouraging at home then at church and extending to the community. Mentors are encouragers!

CHAPTER SIX REVIEW

DISCUSSING ISSUES

1. What does the word encouragement mean?

   To look to someone's potential, beyond failures to see an instrument of the Most High.

2. Why is there a notable absence of encouragement in the home and church?

   Lack of vision, staying in the present judgement.

3. How have others made an impact on your life through encouragement?

   Aunt Judy, aunt Kathrine & aunt Margaret looked beyond the superficial beauty & saw a tender heart for God.

STUDYING GOD'S WORD

4. Consider this passage: *"When [Barnabas] arrived and <u>saw the evidence of the grace of God</u>, he was glad and encouraged them all to remain true to the Lord with all their hearts. He was a good man, full of the Holy Spirit and faith, and a great number of people were brought to the Lord"* (Acts 11:23-24).

   What is the grace of God?

   God's redemptive act by Christ's example

   Unwarranted love of a Father for his children.

What are the qualities of Barnabas that made him an effective encourager?

He saw beyond the deeds of man & knew what the Lord could do with a malleable heart & mind & life.

What is evidence of being "full of the Holy Spirit" according to this passage?

His faith in God to move mountains + to shake His people towards the Truth of the gospel.

5. Review five ways Barnabas showed encouragement as a mentor in the following passages. Suggest personal applications of each of these principles.

way	application
Acts 4:36-37 *Knew all he owned was a gift from God*	*Bring the proceeds into the work of God*
Acts 9:27-28 *Barnabas defended Paul's telling of his vision & the hope put upon him.*	*Gear-up together & be of "one accord"*
Acts 11:22-26 *Barnabas - stay true in your hearts, target*	*Pair up with reliable witnesses*
Acts 15:37-38 *w/ Paul Barn + Paul argued over taking Mark on a mission*	*Know God works thru conflicts & disagreements*
Acts 13:2 and 13:42 *13:2 Dedicated Paul + Barn. for a special purpose. 13:42 Belief in the unbelievable God's gift of salvation*	*Their works + reputation was used to proclaim God's grace. People act for my knowledge + understanding of His life & salvation*

APPLYING GOD'S WORD

6. How can you be an encourager to your family? *believe God's purposes*

   ...to your spouse? *allow time for reflection + point to God's grace + unconditional love.*

   ...to your children? *Show a forgiving heart + cherish their time.*

7. How can you be more encouraging to your church leadership? What can you specifically do to encourage your pastor?

   send a e-mail

8. How can you be a more effective encourager at work?

KEY VERSE:

Memorize and meditate on Acts 11:23-24.

When he arrived & saw the evidence of the grace of God, he was glad & encouraged them all to remain true to the Lord w/ all their hearts. He was a good man, full of the Holy Spirit & faith and a great many people were brought to the Lord.

Part 2
Examples of Mentoring

CHAPTER SEVEN

The Method of the Master

The Lord Jesus is the Supreme Mentor. He exemplified for us the process of mentoring in his selection and training of the apostles. He showed us how to transfer spiritual truths, character traits and ministry skills to others.

Robert E. Coleman writes in *The Master Plan of Evangelism*, "Jesus' concern was not with programs to reach the multitudes, but with men whom the multitudes would follow . . . Men were His method of winning the world to God."[50] Jesus concentrated his efforts on a few.

From a human perspective, Jesus' disciples were "unschooled and ordinary men" (Acts 4:13). They were, however, teachable and available. The Lord's strategy was to instruct these few men and to endue them with authority. Through their lives and message, the Lord sought to reach the world (John 17:6, 9, 17, 20).

Building Trust

The Lord initiated the mentoring relationship by building trust in himself. One way he cultivated that confidence in himself was by performing miraculous signs. According to John 2:11, "The first of his miraculous signs, Jesus performed in Cana of Galilee. He thus revealed his glory, and his disciples put their faith in [*episteusan eis*] him."

The Apostle John's use of the verb *pisteuo* with the preposition *eis* is significant in understanding the kind of trust Jesus is seeking to build. Literally, the expression *pisteuo eis* means to "believe into." This expression means more than believing facts about a person in the sense of an intellectual judgment. It includes the element of personal trust.

Pisteuo followed by *eis* finds its roots in the Hebrew words *'aman b'*. It has the moral element of personal trust or reliance inherent in the Hebrew phrase.[51] "Faith, for John, is an activity which takes men right out of themselves and makes them one with Christ."[52]

Therefore, faith or trust is a strongly interpersonal activity. A mentor's competence and character are a catalyst for building the protégé's confidence and trust.

Spending Time Together

Jesus modeled mentoring by spending time with his disciples. Jesus began the discipleship process with the invitation, "Come, follow me" or literally "Come after me" (*deute opiso mou*, Mark 1:17). He summoned his disciples to join him in sharing his life and ministry (Mark 1:17; 2:14; 3:14; and 6:7).

From the larger group of disciples, Jesus selected his apostles so that "they might be with him" (from *'osin met' autou*, Mark 3:14). This expression "always includes being in the physical presence or in the company of someone . . . The Twelve, therefore, were given a special personal relationship with Jesus . . ."[53]

After a busy day of serving, the Lord invited his apostles to spend some quiet time with him. Jesus said, "Come with me by yourselves to a quiet place and get some rest" (Mark 6:31b). Later, even in the most difficult hours of his life in the Garden of Gethsemene, Jesus brought three of his apostles with him to learn from those moments about the grace of God and the strength he provides (Mark 14:32-33).

You will notice that Jesus mentored his disciples in the small group setting. The Lord spent time with the twelve and then with the three. Mentoring is not always a one-on-one relationship. It can also flourish within a small group of people committed to mutual encouragement.

> The essence of the Lord's training program was not a manual of information. It was the example of his life.

Sharing Your Heart

Jesus' model of mentoring included self-disclosure. He affirmed: "You are my friends, if you do what I command. I no longer call you servants, because a servant does not know his master's business. Instead, I call you friends, for everything I learned from my Father I have made known to you" (John 15:14-15). Such self-disclosure indicates one's trust in those to whom you are talking. With self-disclosure comes vulnerability.

Showing How

The essence of the Lord's training program was not a manual of information. It was the example of his life. Jesus himself was the school and the curriculum. For example, Jesus taught his disciples how to pray after they watched his life of prayer (Luke 11:1-4).

The best way to learn plumbing is to be a plumber's helper. The best way to learn to be an electrician is to work with a master electrician. The best way to learn teaching is to be a student teacher under a master teacher. The best way to learn marketing is to travel with a successful salesman. The best way to learn to be a leader in ministry is to minister with an accomplished leader. The best way to learn parenting is to spend time with godly dads and moms. The best way to learn life is from a godly mentor. That is because we learn best from examples.

Giving Responsibility

"After this the Lord appointed seventy-two others and sent them two by two ahead of him to every town and place where he was about to go" (Luke 10:1). After Jesus demonstrated ministry, he released his disciples to do ministry themselves. He delegated responsibilities so that the disciples implemented what he taught them. He wanted to equip and to empower them to become "fishers of men."

It may be easier to do the work ourselves. We may be more proficient. Doing the task ourselves may be more efficient in the short run. However, that method will not multiply ministry. Only when we release work through others can we expand the work. Effective mentoring releases the protégé to multiply ministry.

Supervising Progress

"The apostles gathered around Jesus and reported to him all they had done and taught" (Mark 6:30). Jesus delegated work then followed-up on what was accomplished.

How often do we recruit a new person for a task and then leave them fumbling? If we assign some work we need to plan adequate time for supervision. Supervision requires time, understanding, patience and clarification. Success and failure are both part of the learning process. The Lord taught by showing how, giving responsibility and supervising progress.

Committing to One Another

Jesus said to his disciples, "If anyone would come after me, he must deny himself and take up his cross and follow me" (Mark 8:34b). Jesus demonstrated commitment to his disciples. However, an effective protégé must reciprocate in commitment and concentration. A mentoring relationship requires personal sacrifice (Luke 14:33). Few are willing to pay that price (John 6:67-69).

My dad (Peter's) grew up on a farm in Narragansett, Rhode Island. He was the son of a tenant farmer who was the caretaker for the estate of two wealthy Bostonian families. In our conversations, Dad would often use farming analogies. He said, "You can lead a horse to water, but you can't make him drink." That is, there must be determination and dedication on the part of the protégé to benefit from the mentor's guidance.

Caring

Finally, Jesus was the Supreme Mentor because he was the Supreme Sacrifice. "Greater love has no one than this, that he lay down his life for his friends" (John 15:13). Jesus demonstrated loving concern for his protégés. That is the essence of a mentoring relationship.

Following the Example of the Lord Jesus

One winter's day in December of 1741, Samuel Hopkins arrived at the parsonage of Jonathan and Sarah Edwards in Northhampton, Massachusetts. A graduate of Yale University, Samuel pursued an internship by going to live with the Edwards. Ministerial students often boarded at the parsonage on King Street. These young men wanted to learn from the example of an experienced and respected minister and from the counsel of his godly wife.

Under Rev. Edward's mentoring, Samuel grew in his personal life, theological understanding, and ministry skills. This apprentice recalled being impressed by his mentor's "abiding sense of divine things on his mind and of constantly living in the fear of God."[54] Samuel observed his mentor's "uncommon thirst for knowledge." Edwards commonly spent thirteen hours of every day in his study where "he searched the Scriptures and helped those who sought his counsel."[55]

The young ministry student watched how Jonathan Edwards invested time in the lives of his own children. Samuel observed, "Before the family entered into the business of the day, he attended on family prayers, when a chapter of the Bible was read . . . upon which he asked his children questions according to their age and capacity."[56] In the evening the family relaxed together in the parlor after tea. It was also Edward's custom to take one of his children with him on horseback on journeys away from home.

Samuel observed Jonathan Edward's great capacity for deep and trusting friendship. In spite of all the commitments of his ministry, this minister would give time for "private meetings" with his protégés. Edward's "known and tried friends always found him easy of access, kind and condescending; and though not talkative, yet affable and free. Among such whose candor and friendship he had experienced, he threw off the reserve, and was most open and free."[57]

On several occasions, Edwards would entrust his pulpit to this ministry student. He showed confidence in his student. He delegated responsibility and released his protégé into ministry.

"As with other men who stayed at the parsonage, a bond was to develop between Edwards and Hopkins which endured for a life. There were to be many other visits by Hopkins to Northhampton following the six or seven months which he spent there in 1741-42."[58] These mentoring relationships with ministerial students became life long associations.

Summary

The nature of the mentoring relationship is stated simply in Jesus' invitation, "Come, follow me . . . and I will make you fishers of men" (Mark 1:17). "Come, follow me . . ." Mentoring involves spending time with the mentor—to know Christ. "And I will make you . . ." Mentoring involves being transformed into the likeness of the mentor—to become like Christ. "Fishers of men." Mentoring empowers the disciple to introduce others to Christ. By being with the Lord, mentoring involves transformation into his character and empowerment for his service.

Jonathan Edwards followed the Lord Jesus' example of mentoring. Edwards invested time in the lives of students. He invited them into his home, cared for them, and shared his heart. He demonstrated ministry before his students, delegated responsibilities to them and supervised their progress. This ministerial training was more personal and holistic than formal classroom training. The mentor's concern was for the development and equipping of the whole person for ministry.

CHAPTER SEVEN REVIEW

DISCUSSING ISSUES

1. What are the advantages of mentoring in the context of small accountability groups in contrast to one-on-one mentoring relationships?

    One on one is good in the beginning when walking w/ the Lord, but a small group is better since many help carry a light load.

2. Why did Jesus focus on a few men rather than the multitudes?

    He instructed a few men to endow them w/ the riches of his life & then expected them to do the same.

STUDYING THE BIBLE

3. What kind of faith is the basis of the Christian's relationship with Christ? (John 2:11)

    Jesus reveals his glory & then people put their faith in him, His miracles.

4. In addition to the miraculous signs, what other ways did Jesus cultivate his disciples trust in himself?

    He showed his vunerability to them being entrapped in a human body w/ its needs but still able to call upon the father for his power and strength.

5. Read the following passages. What quality of Jesus' mentoring is found in each passage?

    Matthew 10:1 *drive out evil spirits & heal 1. Miracles*

    Mark 2:14 *"follow me" 2. Instruction*

    Mark 3:14 *selects + empowers 3. Gave Authority*

    Mark 6:30-31 *disciples were accountable & Jesus - Gave Rest*

    Mark 8:34 *deny yourself + follow Jesus - commit, trust, surrender*

Mark 14:32-33 _sorrow_

Luke 10:1 _appoints + sends before - Delegates_

John 15:12 _Jesus tells + then gives Joy_

John 15:14-15 _reaches all - call all disciples friends - Inclusiveness_

APPLYING GOD'S WORD

5. Jesus modeled self-disclosure. What hinders us from revealing our hearts to others? When is it appropriate to share?

Fear of ridicule -
after building trust and discovering the
person keeps confidentiality

6. In what ways did Jonathan Edwards follow the example of Christ in training ministry students? _Spent time, opened his home, work efforts + heart to his students,_

7. How could we apply Jesus' example of training in the home, church and workplace?

Come follow me - Open your relationships
to others telling how Jesus provide for
you + pray they find His life in theirs

KEY VERSE:

Meditate on and memorize Mark 1:17.

Come follow me + I will make
you fishers of men.

CHAPTER EIGHT

My Pastor My Mentor

The Apostle Paul was passionate about preaching the Gospel to those who had never heard and committed to mentoring those who were younger in the ministry. As I (Peter) reflect on the life of Rich Ainsworth, my pastor during my latter high school years, he shared those passions—to preach and to mentor. As Paul mentored Timothy so Rich has mentored me.

As Paul journeyed across the rugged terrain of Asia Minor on his second missionary trip, he chose Timothy to join his team.

> Paul came to Derbe and then to Lystra, where the disciple named Timothy lived, whose mother was a Jewess and a believer, but whose father was a Greek. The brothers at Lystra and Iconium spoke well of him. Paul wanted to take him along on the journey (Acts 16:1-3a).

A Mentor Sees Potential in His Protégé

Timothy had liabilities as a potential protégé. He was naturally timid and fearful (1 Cor. 16:10; 2 Tim. 1:7). Having grown up in a rural area he may have lacked sophistication. His spiritual heritage was divided in that he had a Greek father and a Jewish mother. Timothy was not particularly robust in health as evidenced by Paul prescribing a medicinal treatment for his frequent stomach ailments (1 Tim. 5:23). He was young and inexperienced (1 Tim. 4:12). However, the believers "spoke well of him" (Acts 16:2). This good reputation extended from his hometown of Lystra to the town of Iconium some eighteen miles away.

I (Peter) can identify with Timothy's shortcomings. I was very timid. One morning in elementary school I was so afraid of public speaking that I feigned a stomachache to avoid leading the pledge of allegiance at the beginning of the school day. Picture my insurmountable challenge. All I needed to do was to stand in front of the class, place my hand over my heart, and say, "I . . ." The class would then join me in reciting the pledge of allegiance. My mother suspected my pretense but let me stay home. When I arrived at school the next day the teacher said, "Peter missed the opportunity to lead the pledge of allegiance yesterday, let's have him lead today." Sure enough, I lived through the trauma!

Paul learned from his own mentor, Barnabas, not to focus on past failures and possible limitations of his protégé. Instead, Paul focused on Timothy's current progress and future potential. Some of the apprentice's limitations, such as his divided religious background, actually became assets for ministry in that Paul was seeking to reach both the Jews and the Gentiles.

A Mentor Spends Time With His Protégé

Paul's selection of Timothy instilled confidence in him. This formed the foundation for an effective mentoring relationship. The heart of Paul's mentoring relationship with Timothy was found in the short phrase "take him along" or "with him" (KJV, Acts 16:3). Paul was willing to spend time with Timothy modeling ministry for him. Timothy was trained "on the job." This plan is reminiscent of the Lord empowering his apostles. Jesus "appointed twelve—designating them apostles—that they might be *with* him and that he might send them out to preach" (Mark 3:14b).

A Mentor Models His Message

Paul lived the theology he taught. He practiced what he preached. Paul declared, "Follow my example, as I follow the example of Christ" (1 Cor. 11:1). Timothy learned about the sovereignty of God and the leading of the Holy Spirit as they traveled together across Asia Minor. The young man saw the apostle respond to the "Macedonian call" to proclaim the Gospel to the Europeans. Timothy learned how to share the Gospel watching Paul witness to Lydia in Philippi. The protégé observed how to persevere in the face of persecution in Philippi and again in Thessalonica.

Why was Paul an effective mentor? Why would Timothy also become an effective mentor? An effective mentor models his message. Paul later challenged Timothy, "Don't let anyone look down on you because you are young, but set an example for the believers in speech, in life, in love, in faith and in purity" (1 Tim. 4:12).

A Mentor Gives His Protégé Opportunities to Grow

In Berea, Timothy executed his first responsibilities independent of the Apostle. Just as Jesus sent out his disciples two by two, Paul sent Timothy out with a fellow student named Silas. Together they were responsible to oversee the initial development of the church in Berea.

Apparently Timothy completed his work in Berea and joined Paul in Athens where he was promptly sent out on a second assignment. This was the more challenging task of strengthening and encouraging the persecuted church in Thessalonica (1 Thess. 3:1-3). Timothy returned to Paul while the apostle was proclaiming the Gospel in Corinth.

A third assignment for Timothy was when Paul, who was now on his third missionary journey, sent both him and Erastus from Ephesus to strengthen the churches in Macedonia (Acts 19:22). A fourth assignment was a journey from the same city, Ephesus, to reinforce the Apostle Paul's teaching to the Corinthian church (1 Cor. 4:17; 16:10).

From prison in Rome, Paul promised to send Timothy on another assignment to assist the church in Philippi (Phil. 2:19-24). At this point in their ministry together, Paul describes Timothy as "like-minded" (v. 20). John Walvoord sees in this expression the element of bonding in their relationship. "The word translated 'like-minded' is found only here in the New Testament and literally is 'like-souled' . . . Of all Paul's converts, Timothy seemed to have manifested the greatest faithfulness to the Lord as well as fidelity to Paul."[59]

Later still Timothy was instructed to stay in Ephesus to strengthen the church there (1 Tim. 1:3). In Ephesus Timothy was the man in charge and not simply an emissary for the Apostle Paul. Timothy had matured in ministry under the tutelage of Paul so that he was now in leadership.

Paul's final request of Timothy was an appeal for him to come visit him during his second imprisonment and to be a source of encouragement to him (2 Tim. 4:9). Timothy has been called a "postage stamp" because he always stuck to the mission on which he was sent. He had grown in character and ministry effectiveness as he "followed closely" his mentor's life and teaching (1 Tim. 4:6).

A Mentor Really Cares

Paul frequently referred to Timothy in terms of endearment such as "my true son. . ." (1 Tim. 1:2) and "my dear son . . ." (2 Tim. 1:2). A mentor must have a sincere and sacrificial concern for the wellbeing of others. Essential to effective mentoring is genuine concern for the protégé.

Paul's letter to the Philippian believers confirms Timothy's readiness for mentoring others because of his protégé's concern for others. Paul wrote: "I hope to send Timothy to you soon, that I also may be cheered when I receive news about you. I have no one else like him, who takes a genuine interest in your welfare. For everyone looks out for his own interests, not those of Jesus Christ" (Phil 2:19-20).

A Mentor is Faithful

Paul was an effective mentor because he was "considered . . . faithful" (1 Tim. 1:12). Faithfulness is a quality that Paul believed also authenticated Timothy's readiness to mentor. Timothy had "proved" (*dokime*) himself fit and trustworthy (Phil. 2:19-22). That is, through testing he demonstrated reliability. And when seeking church leaders, Paul instructed Timothy to look for trustworthy men (2 Tim. 2:2).

A Mentor Like Paul in My Life

As Paul was to Timothy, so Rich Ainsworth was to me (Peter). As a mentor, he was "a brain to pick, a shoulder to cry on, and a kick in the pants."

I was a junior in high school when Rich, a young Dallas Theological Seminary graduate, arrived in my home town of Bloomfield, Connecticut to pastor a new church. At that time, the church consisted of a small nucleus of believers that met in the basement of a house. As Paul was directed to a spiritually needy Europe through the "Macedonian call," so Rich responded to a "New England call."

Prior to that time, my family had traveled to another community to attend church. However, my parents wanted a local church where we could invite friends, classmates, neighbors and co-workers to join us. So we began to worship with this young Wintonbury Church. When we first arrived, our family of eight doubled the size of some services we attended.

This young pastor surprised me. He didn't wear a black suit. In retrospect, I'm quite certain he didn't own one. The church family didn't call him Reverend or Pastor Ainsworth, he was simply "Rich." I could relate to him. He played on the church softball team, mowed the lawn, wore jeans and enjoyed basketball. He was a pastor without a halo!

Soon Rich and Kathy's living room was overflowing with fifty or more students, larger than the Sunday morning worship attendance at that time. Students would play their guitars accompanying, "We are one in the Spirit . . . and Kum Ba Yah . . ." Sounds like the 70's, doesn't it? Rich taught the youth group Bible study one evening each week. I was impressed that I could understand what the Bible said and how I should apply it.

Rich helped me to understand evangelism as a lifestyle. I had thought evangelism was a program—going door to door leaving Gospel tracts or wearing a pin to prompt questions. Rich and Kathy built relationships with those who did not know Christ so as to build trust. People accepted the message because of the credibility of the messengers.

Other denominational pastors would ask Rich how he had such a successful youth ministry. The answer was peers reaching peers for Christ. He invested his life in youth leaders who would reach their peers for Christ. Friends came because of friends and stayed because Rich invested time in sharing biblical truth with them. Ray Lagan, who is now an elder at Wintonbury Church, came to Christ through the witness of that youth group.

After school I would bicycle over to ask Rich to "shoot some hoop" in the neighborhood park across from the church. I figured that pastors played basketball with high school kids. Sure enough, he put down his sermon preparation and joined me. I would ask questions and share my struggles. Rich was a "shoulder to cry on."

I wanted to become "just like Rich." He was a model and a motivator—a mentor. Rich showed me the pastor's life in a practical, everyday manner. Rich's example and investment in my life inspired me to follow in his steps. During my senior year in high school, because of Rich's example and the Spirit's leading, I felt the prompting to pursue the pastoral ministry.

> A mentor gives his protégé opportunities for ministry, helps open doors, and releases him to serve.

During my senior year I was President of the National Honor Society at the local public high school. I invited Rich to open the induction ceremony with prayer. He prayed in Jesus' Name. I was impressed with his courage; but I got in trouble with the school administration.

When the vice-principal asked me to deliver the academic speech at the high school graduation ceremony, I was told I could speak on any subject I wanted to—except Jesus Christ. Following Rich's example I responded in this way, "If I am to give the graduation speech I will need to be given the freedom to speak on any subject I should choose." The vice-principal conceded.

As I prepared the speech, I often asked Rich for advice. I practiced in the church auditorium over and over again. Rich was "a brain to pick." At the graduation ceremony I challenged the graduates "to consider the claims of Christ when running the marathon of life."

When the Lord spoke to my heart to go to seminary, where would I go? I wanted to learn to understand and teach the Bible "just like Rich." Of course, it would be where Rich went to school. I sought a seminary where I could learn to teach the Bible like Rich could. Rich loved God's Word, learned it, lived it and taught it.

When the Lord brought Rhonda into my life, who was I going to talk to about preparation for marriage? It would be Rich and Kathy. They modeled a marriage that I wanted to have. They counseled us about marriage.

A mentor gives his protégé opportunities for ministry . . . helps open doors . . . and releases him to serve. When I returned home from school on breaks Rich gave me opportunities to help with church ministry. As I concluded seminary I received a call from Don Smith, Senior Pastor at First

Baptist Church in Narragansett, Rhode Island, my Dad's home church. Pastor Don was looking for a youth pastor and Rich Ainsworth, who was vacationing in Rhode Island, recommended me to Don for the position. Rich helped me find my first full-time pastoral ministry opportunity. And Pastor Don was a "pastor's pastor" who helped me learn skills in ministry.

Rich's model of faithfulness was a "kick in the pants" when my ministry became difficult and I wanted to quit. When ministry got tough I would call Rich for perspective and encouragement. As my mom and dad invested in my life and provided an anchor for my emotional strength, so Rich's example of faithfulness in ministry has been an anchor for me in pastoral ministry.

As the ministry at Wintonbury Church has grown, Rich has understood the principle Paul gave to Timothy when he said, "The things you have heard me say in the presence of many witnesses entrust to reliable men who will be qualified to teach others" (2 Tim. 2:2). Thus over these last few years, the home support groups have developed with Rich investing in the lives of the leaders of these groups.

Summary

Rich recently retired after 40 years of faithful service in pastoral ministry at Wintonbury Church. This length of service is rare. Effective ministry takes time. Mentoring also requires faithfulness. Paul's greatest qualification for ministry and mentoring was that "he fought the good fight . . . finished the race . . . kept the faith" (2 Tim. 4:7). Paul placed a premium on faithfulness.

CHAPTER EIGHT REVIEW

DISCUSSING ISSUES

1. How should a mentor treat the protégé's weaknesses? How should the mentor approach issues that need to be changed?

   Expedite confidence in replacing fear w/ faith knowing your protégé w/ God's help will overcome. Approach issues that need to be changed w/ prayer (let them know you are praying, + compassion)

STUDYING GOD'S WORD

2. What were the qualities of Paul that made him an effective mentor? (Consider Acts 16:1-3; 1 Corinthians 11:1; 1 Timothy 1:2,12; and 2 Timothy 1:2.)

   1. People speak well of him
   2. Follow Christ's example - pure heart of love
   3. avoid myths + controversy - avoiding simple nature
   *   a faithful appointment*
   4. Have Grace, Mercy, Peace fr. God the Father & J.C. our Lord

   Grace) Mercy) peace)

3. What were Timothy's liabilities? How did God use these liabilities to accomplish his work? (See 1 Corinthians 16:10; 1 Timothy 4:12; 5:23; and 2 Timothy 1:7)

   Timothy was young
   do not despise His youth
   use a little wine because of stomach ailments
   God didn't give a spirit of - He gave power, love + self discipline -
   Timidity

4. How did Paul prepare and empower Timothy for ministry? (See Acts 19:22; 1 Corinthians 4:17 and 16:10; Philippians 2:19-24; 1 Thessalonians 3:1-3; 1 Timothy 1:3; 4:6 and 2 Timothy 4:9.)

   Give direction, + send two by two
   come quickly when called

APPLYING GOD'S WORD

5. How did "Rich" reflect Paul's model of a mentor?

   Smart + knowledgeable
   Sympathetic + tender
   Firm + leading w/ a "kick in the pants"

6.   Which of these qualities of a mentor do you want to develop in your life?

tenderness

7.   Who has invested in your life like a Paul and like my mentor Rich?

Joan Gobel, Lucille, Diane, Joyce Meyers, Gail

KEY VERSE:

Meditate on and memorize Philippians 2:19-20.

Send quickly someone who takes a genuine interest in your welfare.

CHAPTER NINE

Mentoring By a Father-in-law

Sometimes in-laws are called "outlaws," but not in the life of a man named Moses. Moses found his father-in-law, Jethro, to be a wise and caring mentor who provided insights about life and leadership. From his own experience, Jethro helped empower Moses to achieve his God-ordained goals.

During my (Peter's) freshman year in high school, my future father-in-law, Dr. Ronald Nasshan, was called to pastor my home church, Calvary Church, then meeting in Hartford, Connecticut. I was fifteen years old and so was his daughter, Rhonda. I was impressed by his preaching, his wife's spiritual wisdom—and by his daughter's good looks!

My relationship with my future in-laws had a rough start. Although we shared a commitment to Christ, our family histories, personalities and lifestyles were very different. My family was informal and spontaneous which is a nice way of saying disorganized! Her family was formal and well planned. Every time I visited her home as a high school student, the house was spotless. If you visited my home, well, with six kids the house was not tidy! Opposites do attract!

Just as the hinge on a door feels stress when joining the door and the frame, so a wedding experiences the stress of two family histories joining together. Our contrasting family personalities created friction throughout the wedding planning. With friction came heat! I naively suggested that the groomsmen should wear blue blazers and gray slacks rather than tuxedos. That was a practical and economical decision, so I thought. My in-laws disagreed; we wore tuxedos!

Those early difficulties in my relationship with my father-in-law helped me appreciate the reconciliation and relationship we later enjoyed. Stressful experiences can lead to significant personal growth. Both my father-in-law and I determined to strengthen our relationship.

During my early years of pastoral ministry, I sought out my father-in-law for insight. For more than twenty-five years, he had traveled the road upon which I was setting out and I wanted to learn from his experience. Our families would meet together on Mondays, our shared day off. The mentoring "classroom" was often a walk in the mall. Hours seemed to pass by like minutes. I talked. He listened. He spoke about the doctrines of grace and the struggles of ministry, and I learned. My father-in-law showed love, acceptance and patience, crucial qualities of a mentor. "Dad" had a tender heart. He didn't have quick answers or harsh judgments. He affirmed me and gave me hope.

During my first years as a point man on the battlefield of pastoral ministry I engaged in skirmishes with one of my church's trustees. I'll call him "Ralph." After one morning service Ralph called me at the parsonage and criticized the "radical" change I had introduced in the order of worship. Angrily he attacked, "You read the Scripture *after* you prayed rather than *before* you prayed!" Imagine how this man would have responded if I had introduced Willow Creek Church's seeker-sensitive worship style to our congregation!

Simply, Ralph didn't like me. His attitude of distrust was rooted in a long history of bad relationships with pastors. The more I tried to understand and befriend him, the more he attacked what he perceived to be my weaknesses and vulnerability. He insisted that I find another ministry. When

I did not respond promptly to his request, he announced that he would call for a vote of confidence to remove me from the pastorate at the next quarterly business meeting.

Feeling assaulted by uncertainty and fear, I called my father-in-law. On the cold winter night of the church business meeting, my mentor and friend drove three hours to be at the church. When he arrived, he prayed with me. Then he promised, "I will be in your office praying for you during the meeting."

The Lord intervened in an extraordinary way that evening. During the course of the business meeting my pastoral intern, Rob Sundholm, shared his quarterly ministry report. He spoke with passion and conviction about the Lord's work in his life through the ministry of the church. As he spoke there was a special sense of God's presence. The Spirit of God melted cold hearts on that snowy winter night.

The hour was past midnight, but my father-in-law traveled home for his own ministry responsibilities the next morning. His caring encouragement is the kind of stuff that makes mentors and strengthens protégés.

The Lord intervened that night through two significant people. My father-in-law was my mentor who inspired and prayed for me. My protégé showed what ministry is all about.

Soon the entire leadership of the church recognized the destructive and divisive pattern of the irate trustee. The deacons, our spiritual leaders, called Ralph in to a leadership meeting to be corrected. During the discipline session he warned me, "In two weeks you will not be able to officiate at the communion service because your heart is not right with God." I acknowledged my imperfections, but insisted that our motivation for correcting him was because we loved him and the church.

Communion Sunday morning came and Ralph did not arrive. I received a phone call after the service. He was in the hospital having suffered a massive heart attack that morning. He never returned to the church. God intervened. God protected his church. I discovered firsthand the power of both a mentor and a protégé in my life.

Mentoring sessions typically do not take place in the sterile environment of the classroom. It is in the rough and tumble of life that we learn wisdom from caring models. We often learn best from those who have traveled a road similar to the one we plan to journey.

A Mentor Models His Message

Moses' father-in-law, Jethro, also showed the qualities of a mentor. He gave insight concerning life and leadership. As a more experienced person, Jethro helped empower Moses with abilities to meet needs and to achieve goals.

> **Words have an impact if they are propelled by an exemplary life.**

In the process of mentoring, who you are precedes what you say. Words have an impact if they are propelled by an exemplary life.[60] Jethro was a shepherd who was called the "priest of Midian" (Exod. 2:16; 3:1). The title "priest" showed his spiritual character and leadership in the Midianite community. Jethro was also referred to as "Reuel" which means "Friend of God" (Exod. 2:18).

Joe Bastion, a merchant marine retiree, once shared this story. His ship's chief officer gave a compelling speech to the young crew just before embarking at their first port stop. The officer knew that these men were vulnerable to temptation because they were a long way from home. The leader warned his subordinates about the impending temptations found in a seaside resort.

"Be careful," warned the chief officer, "Don't drink too much. Avoid prostitutes!" At the conclusion of his emotional appeal he conceded, "Do as I say, not as I do." Ouch! His entire challenge was deflated because his walk did not match his words.

How many times have you found an articulate, accurate and even passionate message unconvincing because you did not respect the character of the speaker? Whether that communicator is a military officer, CEO, pastor, salesperson, politician or parent, respect for the speaker gives persuasive power to his or her words.

After Moses killed the Egyptian slave master, he fled from Egypt to Midian. There he met Jethro's seven daughters while they were trying to get water for their flocks. Other shepherds were bullies, keeping all the water for themselves. Moses intervened and protected Jethro's daughters and helped water their animals.

Jethro invited Moses to live with his family. Moses was given one daughter, Zipporah, to be his wife. Jethro established credibility with Moses by how he lived day in and day out (Exod. 2:20-21). During those shepherding years a relationship grew between Moses and his father-in-law who modeled for Moses the principles and patterns of life he wanted his protégé to develop. Jethro earned respect and trust from his protégé (Exod. 18:7).

A Mentor Propels the Protégé into Opportunities

After Moses' encounter with God at the burning bush, Jethro released him from his shepherding responsibilities and encouraged him to return to Egypt to help the Israelites. Moses went back to Jethro his father-in-law and said to him, "Let me go back to my own people in Egypt to see if any of them are still alive." Jethro said, "Go, and I wish you well (*shalom*)" (Exod. 4:18).

Moses obtained his father-in-law's permission to depart with his family. In those patriarchal days the extended family was under the father-in-law's authority.[61] As a true mentor, Jethro liberated Moses to fulfill his God-given potential.

Jethro encouraged Moses to develop his abilities and maximize the use of his talents. He released him to "attempt great things for God and expect great things from God." Jethro was secure about himself. This mentor encouraged his protégé to excel beyond his own accomplishments.

A Mentor Listens Before Speaking

When Moses was later reunited with Jethro after Israel's exodus from Egypt, he expressed great respect toward his father-in-law (Exod. 18:7).[62] Out of respect for the mentor, a protégé will seek the elder's advice, follow his example, reflect his character, and be inspired by his encouragement.

Moses enjoyed open communication with Jethro (Exod. 18:8). Moses poured out stories about his recent experiences including both the trials and the blessings. Jethro was for Moses a "brain to pick" and a "shoulder to cry on."

Richard Tyre's research has emphasized the importance of the mentor listening to the personal needs and concerns of the protégé. This attentiveness, he believes, is crucial to building trust that is foundational to the mentoring relationship.[63] Active listening reveals concern about the other person. Excessive talking by a potential mentor shows that he cares more about himself and his own ideas.

Jethro's attentiveness was an outstanding quality of an effective mentor. He listened before talking. Moses shared his heart and experiences. Then the mentor provided guidance and advice (Exod. 18:7).

A Mentor Protects the Protégé from Pitfalls

Jethro counseled Moses concerning his service as judge for the nearly two million Israelites. Moses described his task: "The people come to me to seek God's will. Whenever they have a dispute, it is brought to me, and I decide between the parties and inform them of God's decrees and laws" (Exod. 18:15).

Perhaps you have had an experience in a court of law. As a pastor, I occasionally accompanied attendees of my church to family court. I can picture Moses' caseload. People stood around from early in the morning until late in the evening to receive the judge's attention. Moses faced the tyranny of the urgent as he responded to the vast needs of a hurting nation.

Jethro bluntly disapproved of Moses' approach (Exod. 18:17). The mentor expressed his conviction and fear that Moses would "wear himself out", as well as the people who had to stand and wait for so long. The same expression was used of wilting leaves and flowers in Psalm 37:2. This was no task for one man.[64]

Jethro counseled Moses to do four things. First, Moses should be a man of prayer by being "the people's representative before God and bring their disputes to him" (Exodus 18:19b). Second, he should instruct the people in God's "decrees and laws" (18:20a). Third, he needs to show by his own example how to live pleasing to God (18:20b). Finally, he counseled Moses to delegate responsibility. These are wise suggestions for every spiritual leader.

A Protégé is Teachable

It is a foolish leader who continues to disregard good guidance. According to Proverbs 1:5, "A wise man seeks counsel." Even at the age of eighty Moses had the good sense to take his father-in-law's advice.[65]

In response to Jethro's insight, Moses delegated responsibility to a leadership team. Delegating responsibility was crucial to his effectiveness as a leader (Exod. 18:22-26). This leadership team included over seventy thousand judges at the various levels. The goal for Moses was not simply to do God's work himself, but to develop the skills of others so they too could know, follow, and serve the Lord.

According to Exodus 18:21, those selected to serve in leadership should have three qualities: (1) reverence for God, (2) trustworthiness (*emet*) of character, and (3) disdain for dishonest gain. The Hebrew term *emet* can mean "steady" or "trustworthy."[66] These qualities of leadership are crucial character traits in the mentor and must be developed in the protégé. They are very applicable today!

Mentoring is not dictatorial. A mentor guides his protégé toward making wise decisions. Jethro told Moses to inaugurate the plan only if God commanded him to do so (Exod. 18:23).[67] Moses was to follow Jethro's instruction on the condition that it was consistent with God's will.

Summary

Jethro, in his relationship to his son-in-law, Moses, showed crucial qualities of a mentor. Jethro modeled his message. He propelled his protégé into new opportunities. He listened before he spoke. He protected his protégé from pitfalls. Moses responded as a teachable protégé to an exemplary mentor.

CHAPTER NINE REVIEW

DISCUSSING ISSUES

1. Why do leaders do tasks themselves rather than training and delegating the work to others?

    Lack of trust that anyone else will do it as good or better.

STUDYING GOD'S WORD

2. How did Jethro show a willingness to help Moses expand his ministry (Exodus 4:18)?

    Let Moses go back to his people in Egypt & wished him well.

3. Why do you believe Moses was ready to accept Jethro's advice about leadership? (Consider Exodus 2:16,18, 20-21; 3:1; and 18:7-9.)

    He rescued Jethro's daughters & sheep. Jethro invited Moses to eat & marry his daughter. Moses worshipped God in the mountain. Moses was an "open book" to Jethro telling him all the hardships & the miracles God performed on their behalf.

4. Describe Moses' responsibilities as a judge in Exodus 18:5 and 6.

    Moses had responsibility not only as a leader but also of sons, wife & father in law.

5. Describe Moses' openness to share with his father-in-law in Exodus 18:8.

    He shared the hardships they encountered describing that even in the worst of time God's protection & provision were with them.

6. What kind of listening skills did Jethro demonstrate (Exodus 18:9-10)?

    Was delighted with the move of God & praised him.

7. Why do you believe Moses was trying to resolve all the disputes among the people of Israel by himself (Exodus 18:13-14)?

    Spent too much time with their complaints & didn't realize need to delegate.

APPLYING GOD'S WORD

8. How could you apply to your own work the four instructions Jethro gave to Moses?

    Exodus 18:19b *Bring disputes to God.*

    18:20a *Teach the Laws & decrees (Love your enemies)*

    18:20b *Show the way to live & duties to be performed*

    18:21 *appoint capable men (women) who reverence God, who are trustworthy who hate dishonest gain,*

9. What aspects of the three qualities of potential leaders given in Exodus 18:21 would you like to develop in your personal life?

    More reverence of God.
    Know your capabilities
    Continue in Trustworthiness

10. What were the responsibilities of these selected leaders (Exodus 18:22)?

    Serve as judge
    Share w/ Moses the difficult cases.

11. Jethro was not dogmatic in his advice to Moses. How can you demonstrate this quality of mentoring (Exodus 18:23)?

    Ways to lighten the load.

KEY VERSE:

Memorize and meditate on Exodus 18:8.

Moses told all the Lord had done & saved them

CHAPTER TEN

Mentoring for Career Development

Business, education, community and church— all kinds of organizations would benefit from mentoring. Mentoring accelerates the skill development of the workforce. Mentoring prepares future leaders for the organization. Bobb Biehl observes: "Mentoring relationships increase the rate of organizational growth, reduce turnover, and maintain organizational stability."[68]

A mentor gives the protégé shoulders to stand on. The more experienced professional helps the less experienced worker reduce the time consuming trial and error method of learning and advancement. The mentor opens opportunities by providing perspective on decisions and personal contacts for resources.

My (Peter's) youngest brother's career in medicine illustrates the value of mentoring. When Preston was a sophomore pre-med student at Gordon College, my mother was babysitting the child of a medical doctor. She told the doctor about my brother's interest in the medical field. The doctor passed Preston's name on to one of the world's most prominent cardiologists, a professor and researcher at the University of Connecticut School of Medicine.

This world-renowned researcher invited my brother to work in his laboratory during the upcoming summer recess. During his time in the laboratory, Preston met regularly with the cardiologist to summarize his scientific findings under the researcher's critical eye.

This mentoring relationship opened tremendous opportunities for this nineteen-year-old. The experienced scientist supervised his student's research and made contacts for him. As a result Preston contributed original research findings to the university by summer's end. When he showed me his first scientific article, all I could understand was his name, listed after his mentor. The rest was "scientific Greek" to me! Each summer thereafter Preston returned to the lab for further research and expanded opportunities for career development accelerated by the reputation and contacts of the cardiologist.

After Preston was graduated from Gordon College, he was admitted to the University of Connecticut School of Medicine's M.D./Ph.D. program due in large part to his research experiences with his mentor. At twenty-five years old Preston had earned his Ph.D. and received a research fellowship from the American Heart Society.

Preston soon received his first appointment as Assistant Professor at the University of Connecticut Medical School. At thirty he was invited to have his own research program and joined the faculty of the MCP-Hahnemann School of Medicine, Allegheny University of the Health Sciences. Preston, and his wife Pam, who is also a scientist, developed a successful research laboratory. Today he is a professor at Harvard Medical School.

Preston recently addressed an international medical conference where the prominent cardiologist was present. In the lecture, Preston gave credit to his mentor. On this occasion, the protégé was the lecturer and the mentor was the listener. After the presentation, the cardiologist approached Preston and commended him for his progress.

As a medical school faculty member, Preston mentors graduate students. He helps the students to develop their rationale for experimentation and to express their findings in appropriate scientific language. He then helps the students make contacts for career development. The catalyst for this mentoring is the goal of an M.D. or Ph.D. However, Preston finds that the conversation and counsel expand beyond the scope of the scientific method. He guides the students through personal problems that impact their lives. Teaching may have a narrow emphasis on academic achievement. Mentoring has a more holistic focus. Mentoring is committed to the development of the whole person.

Reference Power

Preston heard a lecture by an accomplished business professor who asked this question: "What is the crucial factor that gives a person the most power and influence in an organization?" She answered, "It isn't charisma—the power of personality. It isn't the power of authority—such as the CEO who has a high position in the company. It isn't reward power—such as the ability to give a raise. The crucial factor isn't found in coercion—the ability to hurt you by demoting or terminating employment. The most power and influence is not even found in expertise—the knowledge people must have to advance."

The business professor concluded, "The crucial factor that gives a person the most power and influence in an organization is 'reference power.' That is the ability to reference you to the right person at the right time to provide the right resources to meet your need or achieve your goal."

Reference power combines the knowledge and expertise of one person with that of many others. Effective mentoring has reference power. A mentor empowers the protégé by sharing his own expertise. The mentor also helps the protégé contact other people and resources to help him meet a need, solve a problem or to achieve a goal.

Richard Tyre, Director of the Uncommon Individual Foundation, helped mentor me through my doctoral project on mentoring. I was struggling and stumbling through the research and writing. Professor Tyre helped me identify tools for research. He gave perspective on the process. He networked people to assist me. He explained concepts of mentoring which he had already synthesized. He had knowledge and references. Mr. Tyre was an encourager who inspired me to press on in the face of obstacles.

Moses Mentors Joshua

Mentoring was one of God's methods for developing future leaders for the growing nation of Israel. As Moses was a beneficiary of Jethro's effective mentoring, he also transferred spiritual truths and leadership skills to the next generation through mentoring.

Joshua was a promising young man, selected to be Moses' chief assistant. "Joshua son of Nun . . . had been Moses' aide (*mesharet*) since youth (*baghur*, Num. 11:28)." The word translated "youth" describes Joshua as "choice and in the prime of manhood."[69] A mentoring relationship may last for a few years or as in this case, for the lifetime of the mentor. Moses and Joshua shared a forty-year relationship.

Joshua was identified as Moses' "aide" (*mesharet*) which may also mean "servant, helper, assistant or learner" (Num. 11:28; Josh. 1:1). In mentoring terms, a *mesharet* includes characteristics of a protégé. The role of the *mesharet* included a trusted relationship to the master as exemplified in Joseph's relationship to Potiphar. "Joseph found favor in his [Potiphar's] eyes and became his attendant (*mesharet*). Potiphar put him in charge of his household, and he entrusted to his care everything he owned (Gen. 39:4)."

Mentoring was mutually beneficial for Moses and Joshua. Concerning the role of the *mesharet*, Austel writes: "These men would obviously not be menials. In Esther 2:2 the king's 'attendants' (*mesharetan*) stand in relationship close enough so that they have his ear and are able to make suggestions which the king follows."[70] Joshua was Moses' chief assistant. Both the mentor and the protégé grew through the relationship.

For a protégé to have confidence and trust in his mentor, the mentor must evidence skill and competence. Moses fulfilled these qualifications as a mentor to Joshua. Moses exhibited personal maturity, experience in life, leadership skill, and spiritual insight. Joshua sought to learn from his mentor's wisdom.

Spiritual Mentoring

Moses did not simply cultivate a personal relationship with Joshua. A key to Moses' mentoring relationship with Joshua was that he introduced Joshua into a close relationship of trust with the living God. Joshua witnessed the revelation of God to his mentor in the tent of meeting (Exod. 24:12-18). Later, Moses took his protégé with him up Mount Sinai to be in the very presence of God (Exod. 32:7). Moses allowed Joshua to observe his personal experiences with the Lord (Exod. 33:11). Moses exposed Joshua to the Lord's work and word.[71]

Spiritual mentoring is a triangular relationship that centers on the Lord's presence and guidance. Moses revealed his personal and spiritual life to Joshua. Moses exemplified for Joshua what God could do through a life yielded to him.

Reasonable and timely self-disclosure, even concerning spiritual experiences, is fundamental to the effectiveness of a mentoring relationship.

The Process of Mentoring

Moses was with Joshua during his first military encounters (Exodus 17:8-16). Initially, the Lord does not send Joshua into battle alone. Moses was there to guide, encourage, and intercede. Joshua's first victories were with Moses' help. Moses' upheld arms expressed his intercessory ministry on behalf of Joshua. Later Joshua led God's people into battle without his mentor's presence.

Before sending Joshua out on his own, Moses accompanied his protégé in the initial battles and stood with him (See Exod. 17:9 and Deut. 3:21-22). Joshua's earlier experiences in battle, when Moses was present, were a preparation for his future leadership responsibilities in leading God's people in battle in the land of Canaan (Deut. 31:4). Joshua learned to trust Moses and, even more significantly, to trust the Lord during those initial years of service.

God instructed Moses concerning victory in battle and wanted to make sure that his instruction to Moses was transferred to his protégé as well. The work is not finished when the man of God has completed his own assignment; it is crucial that he pass on what he has learned to others. This principle is found in Exodus 17:14: "The Lord said to Moses, 'Write this on a scroll as something to be remembered and make sure that Joshua hears it.'" The great Jewish commentator, Dr. U. Cassuto, interprets this passage in this way: "Recite it in the ears of Joshua, that is, apart from writing it down, teach it to Joshua by heart, so that it may be preserved for generations both in writing and orally."[72]

When I (Peter) was serving as a Senior Pastor in New Jersey, one of my associates was responsible for pastoral visitation. He was exceptionally gifted in encouraging people through an attentive ear and a word of comfort. When he visited, he shared a fitting word from Scripture and lead in prayer.

This associate would report his visitation accomplishments to me at our weekly staff meeting. I commended him for his diligence, but would ask him this question: "Whom did you take with you on your ministry of visitation?" Initially he answered, "No one."

I challenged him, "Your work is not finished until you have trained someone else to be an effective visitor like you are. Then you have multiplied your ministry through others and given them the joy of serving."

One of my present elders, Dale Norris, oversees visitation in our church. Time and time again he invites younger men to join him when he visits a shut-in, serves communion, or prays for the sick. Years ago, he learned visitation from a mature believer and is determined to multiply ministry through others. Each person in ministry—whether you are a preacher or a servant leader, a Sunday School teacher or a youth worker—should mentor others by including them in ministry.

Joshua was later entrusted with the responsibility of leading God's people into victory in the promised land. Moses was responsible to prepare him for the battles ahead. The Lord instructed Moses concerning Joshua: "Commission Joshua, and encourage and strengthen him, for he will lead this people across and will cause them to inherit the land that you will see" (Deut. 3:28).

Moses was also concerned that there not be a vacuum of leadership for overseeing God's people (Num. 27:15-17). Joshua, therefore, was commissioned as Moses' successor. He was ideally suited to the job, having been Moses' assistant for many years (Num. 11:28; Ex. 17:9; 24:13; 32:17). Mentoring prepared Joshua for the work.

Joshua succeeded Moses in leading God's people (Num. 27:18-23). Joshua did so with God's appointment and enabling. Moses modeled for his protégé confidence in what God could do through his life. The Lord promised Joshua, "As I was with Moses, so I will be with you; I will never leave you nor forsake you" (Josh. 1:5).

Summary

Reference power is the key to the mentor empowering his protégé. Not only does the mentor share his own expertise and experiences, he networks his protégé with others.

The goal of mentoring is not to create a relationship of dependency in which the protégé must continue to rely upon the mentor. The most important reference is to the Lord himself. The mentor helps the protégé to find God's strength through the Holy Spirit and God's wisdom through his word. God himself is the right person at the right time to provide the right resources for life's challenges.

The Lord's word to Joshua is a promise for each one of us as we face the challenges and responsibilities of life.

No one will be able to stand against you all the days of your life. As I was with Moses, so I will be with you. I will never leave you nor forsake you.

Be strong and courageous, because you will lead these people to inherit the land I swore to their forefathers to give them. Be strong and very courageous. Be careful to obey all the law my servant Moses gave you; do not turn from it to the right or to the left, that you may be successful wherever you go. Do not let this Book of the Law depart from your mouth; meditate on it day and night, so that you may be careful to do everything written in it. Then you will be prosperous and successful. Have I not commanded you? Be strong and courageous. Do not be terrified; do not be discouraged, for the Lord your God will be with you wherever you go (Joshua 1:5-9).

CHAPTER TEN REVIEW

DISCUSSING ISSUES

1. Give examples of the most important factor in a mentor's power of influence—reference power?

   God will show you
   1 right person
   2 right time
   3 right resources

2. How did the cardiologist help accelerate my brother Preston's career development?

   opening doors of opportunity
   help + encourage insights

STUDYING GOD'S WORD

3. Reflect back on this chapter and identify what made Moses' mentoring of Joshua effective? Consider Exodus 17:8-16 and 24:12-13.

   (Strength – from Holy Spirit)
   (Wisdom – from God's Word)
   Even though you grow weak God will send strength
   truth God gives more tablets of stone

4. Describe how Moses demonstrated the following statement: "The work is not finished when the man of God has completed his assignment; it is necessary that he transfer what he has learned to others." Consider Exodus 17:14 and Deuteronomy 3:28.

   Write it - make sure others hear it,
   Encourage + strengthen

5. How did mentoring strengthen Joshua's confidence to lead God's people? See Joshua 1:5.

   God promises to never leave
   or forsake.

APPLYING GOD'S WORD

6. If a man whom you respected offered his time and his resources to help you reach your professional or ministry goals over the next few years, do you think he would increase your effectiveness and progress? How would he help you avoid or overcome difficulties more effectively?

    Speaking from his experience, + encouragement to stand on God's word + look to the Holy Spirit for strength thru any trials or hindrances

7. In what areas of your life and work would you like a mentor? How could a mentor help you deal with those needs?

    Being able to say no. Explaining how her life tempered demands by others

8. If you had a more experienced man mentor you where you work, how would that increase your loyalty to that organization?

    Two Together is a stronger bond.

9. Can you give some examples of mentoring relationships in your workplace, professional field, or church?

KEY VERSE:

"The Lord said to Moses, 'Write this on a scroll as something to be remembered and make sure that Joshua hears it'" (Exod. 17:14).

Write on a scroll + remember I will completely blot out the memory of amalek from under Heaven. Refresh spiritual leaders

CHAPTER ELEVEN

Examples of Empowering

In William Franklin Graham Jr.'s autobiography, *Just As I Am*, he credited many people with helping him in his personal, spiritual and ministry development. One of those individuals was John Minder. He was a pastor and dean of men at Florida Bible Institute where Billy Graham was a student. Dr. Minder, Billy recalled, gave "a lot of time to each student . . . He saw me for what I was— a spindly farm boy with lots of nail-biting energy, a mediocre academic record, and a zeal to serve the Lord that exceeded my knowledge and skills."[73]

Billy referred to Dr. Minder as "my beloved Florida mentor." He described the mentor-like qualities of his professor in a way that summarizes the heartbeat of a mentor.

> **A mentor doesn't think for his protégé but teaches him how to think for himself.**

I enthusiastically took his courses in pastoral theology and hermeneutics (or Bible interpretation), and I responded instinctively and positively to his gentle counseling approach . . . Instead of resenting his advice, I wanted to hear everything he could tell me about life and service. He did not dictate how to think and what to do; rather, he opened my thinking to consider the perfect trustworthiness of God, and to rest in that.[74]

Dr. Minder didn't control Billy's ministry but lovingly guided him; the mentor didn't think for his protégé but taught him how to think for himself. The mentor didn't draw his protégé to depend on himself but rather on the Lord who alone is perfectly trustworthy.

A mentor provides opportunities for his protégé to grow. The mentor accelerates his professional advancement. He empowers his protégé for ministry. In the early spring of 1937, during the Bible school's Easter break, Dr. Minder invited Billy to accompany him on a trip to northern Florida. During their travels, the dean was invited by his friend Cecil Underwood to preach at the evening service of a small Baptist church.

"No," Dr. Minder answered, "Billy is going to preach."

Billy was stunned. He resisted. He had never preached a formal sermon in front of a church audience. Mr. Underwood and Dr. Minder both laughed.

"We'll pray for you," said Mr. Underwood, "and God will be with you."

"All right," Billy agreed rather hesitantly. What else could he say to the dean of his school? He was so frightened that he spent the night studying and praying instead of sleeping. He borrowed and practiced about four sermons. He felt they each would last at least twenty or thirty minutes.

The church met in a small meeting room. The congregation consisted of about forty folks primarily composed of ranchers and cowboys in overalls. "The song leader, who chewed tobacco, had to go to the door every so often to spit outside!"[75]

Dr. Graham goes on to recall his learning experience:

When the moment came to walk to the pulpit in the tiny Bostwick Baptist Church, my knees shook and perspiration glistened on my hands. I launched into sermon number one. It seemed to be over almost as soon as I got started, so I added number two. And number three. And eventually number four. Then I sat down. Eight minutes— that was all it took to preach all four of my sermons! Was this the stuff of which those marvelous preachers at Florida Bible Institute were made?

Believe it or not, though, when I got back to campus I felt I had grown spiritually through the experience. But at the same time I was concerned: I could not get away from the nagging feeling in my heart that I was being called by God to preach the Gospel. I did not welcome that call. Whatever glimmer of talent Dr. Minder might have thought he saw in me was certainly Raw, with a capital R.[76]

Billy Graham recalled a later experience when he was a twenty year old student at the Bible Institute: "John Minder gave me an incredible opportunity. He needed to spend some time away that summer and asked me to be his summer replacement at the large Tampa Gospel Tabernacle. For six weeks, I would have my own church, preaching at all the regular services and carrying out my pastoral responsibilities."[77]

Dr. Minder's ministry in the life of Billy Graham was that of a mentor. This professor modeled mentoring by trusting in Billy, encouraging him, and opening and expanding opportunities for ministry. In one word, Dr. Minder "empowered" his protégé. Empowerment is the personal growth that takes place through mentoring by enabling the protégé to address a need, achieve an aspiration or develop through a situation.

An Old Testament Example of Empowering

Elijah's relationship with Elisha was similar to Moses relationship with Joshua. Elijah's name, meaning "God is salvation," described the essence of his ministry. His name evoked the memory of Joshua, "The Lord Saves." The Lord gave Elijah someone to continue his work just as he did for Moses. Elisha channeled the covenant blessings to the faithful in Israel just as Joshua brought Israel into the promised land.[78]

At Horeb, the Lord revealed to Elijah who would be his successor to his prophetic ministry. "The Lord said to him, 'Go back the way you came, and go to the Desert of Damascus. When you get there. . . anoint Elisha son of Shaphat from Abel Meholah to succeed you as prophet'" (1 Kings 19:16).

Elijah was instructed to "anoint for a prophet" (*timshah l'nabi'*) Elisha. There is a fourfold theological significance of "anoint" (*mashah*). First, to anoint a person meant to separate for God's service. Second, the anointed one is authorized by God himself and thus is held in "special regard." Third, the anointing is accompanied by God's enablement through his Spirit. And fourth, anointing is associated with the coming promised deliverer, the Messiah.[79]

Elijah fulfilled the instructions given to him by the Lord. As a result of that anointing and calling, Elisha "set out to follow Elijah and become his attendant" (1 Kings 19:21b). Literally, Elisha "went after Elijah and ministered to him." The word translated "ministered" is from the Hebrew verb *sharat* (related to *mesharet*). This was a significant role. One use of *sharat* refers to the personal service rendered to a ruler.[80]

For a period of time, Elisha accompanied Elijah as his protégé, and observed his ministry. Second Kings, chapter two, describes the bond of trust that developed between these two men.

Three times Elisha affirms his loyalty toward his mentor saying, "As surely as the Lord lives and as you live, I will not leave you" (2 Kings 2:2, 4, 6).

The concluding interaction between Elisha and Elijah was intended "primarily for the strengthening of Elisha's faith."[81] The culmination of the mentoring relationship focused on Elijah empowering his protégé for effective service as God's prophet. Elisha petitioned his mentor for a double portion of his spirit (2 Kings 2:9). The loss of the Spirit-filled and empowered prophet must have gripped Elisha's humble heart. He desperately needed spiritual power far beyond his own capabilities to meet the awesome responsibilities of the work ahead of him. Thus, he asked for the firstborn son's inheritance. That is a double portion. He desired that Elijah's mighty power might continue to live through him.

Subsequent to Elijah's translation to heaven, Elisha immediately patterned his ministry after his mentor. For example, "when he struck the water [of the Jordan River], it divided to the right and to the left, and he crossed over" (2 Kings 2:14b; cp. 2:8).

Elijah exemplified a mentoring relationship with his protégé, Elisha. The mentor helped develop his less experienced protégé to his maximum potential. Through this relationship Elisha was empowered with God-given resources for ministry. He was empowered through the mentoring relationship to accomplish more than he could alone.

A New Testament Example of Empowering

The Apostle Paul, who was a recipient of Barnabas' exemplary mentoring, became in turn an effective mentor. One of the less frequently highlighted mentoring relationships in the Bible is that of Paul and Titus. There is a noticeable absence of Paul's associate from the historical record in the Book of Acts. Titus was first mentioned in the Apostle's letter to the Galatians (2:1-3).

Paul's mentoring of Titus involved availability, a core component in developing bonding. The apostle desired time together with his associate. "Do your best to come to me at Nicopolis, because I have decided to winter there" (Titus 3:12). Paul was encouraged and comforted (*parakalesen*) by Titus' presence. "God . . . comforted us by the coming of Titus" (2 Cor. 7:6). This mutuality of encouragement reveals the mutuality in a mentoring relationship. The mentor benefits as much or more than his protégé from the interaction.

Paul's mentoring involved tenderness toward his protégé. Paul addressed his letter: "To Titus, my true son in our common faith." (Titus 1:4). Titus is identified as Paul's "brother" (2 Cor. 2:13). Both time together and genuine concern for one's protégé seal the bond of trust.

Paul's relationship with Titus emphasized trustworthiness. As Dr. Minder was confident in Billy Graham's calling and abilities, and released him to greater ministry opportunities, the Apostle Paul expressed confidence in Titus and released him to an expanded service. Paul's boasting about Titus proved to be true. The protégé demonstrated reliability (2 Cor. 7:14).

Paul's work with Titus was a team ministry (2 Cor. 8:23). Titus was identified as a "partner" and together they were "fellow workers." Titus extended and multiplied the Apostle Paul's ministry. For example, Titus was the apostle's emissary to Corinth. Paul was experiencing a number of frustrating problems with the church at Corinth, and tried to resolve these difficulties through correspondence. Eventually he sent his protégé to attempt a reconciliation and resolution of the difficulties. Titus is mentioned thirteen times in the New Testament, and eight of those occurrences are in Second Corinthians.

Titus found joy in serving the church at Corinth because of their responsiveness to his leadership and teaching (2 Cor. 7:13-15). Paul's protégé helped in the collection of funds from the Corinthian believers for the church in Jerusalem (2 Cor. 8:6). "The heart of Titus" is deeply concerned for the wellbeing of the church (2 Cor. 8:16-17). He did not take advantage of the church, but loved them (2 Cor. 12:18).

Paul instructed Titus about mentoring (Titus 2:3-4). A mentor must be an example to follow. A mentor's teaching addresses the development of the whole person toward maturity in Christ. Paul also instructed Titus about how to be an effective mentor to young men (Titus 2:6-8). The mentoring relationship included encouragement and accountability (v. 6), setting an example in behavior (v. 7), and integrity (*aphthorian*). *Aphthorian* literally means "without corruption" and therefore is translated full of "integrity."[82] A mentor should also be serious about his conversation (v. 8). "Seriousness" refers to outward dignity.[83] Titus is challenged to teach sound doctrine. He should have a faith that reveals itself in obedience (Titus 2:1-5; 3:8).

Titus exhibited important qualities of a protégé. First, he was faithful to the Lord, to the Apostle Paul, and to the churches he served. Second, he was available. He willingly accepted some very difficult assignments including appointments to the complaining Corinthians and the lying Cretans. Third, he was teachable, receiving instruction from the Apostle Paul. Under Paul's coaching, Titus was empowered for expanded ministry. This protégé became an effective servant who multiplied ministry for God's kingdom.

Summary

Dr. Minder and Billy Graham, Elijah and Elisha, and Paul and Titus are examples of mentoring relationships in which the mentor empowers the protégé. In each pair, the mentor shared God-given resources to enable the protégé to serve the Lord more effectively. The mentor's ministry continued and multiplied through his protégé.

CHAPTER ELEVEN REVIEW

DISCUSSING ISSUES

1. What characteristics of Billy Graham's professor, Dr. Minder, made him an effective mentor?

   Willing to take a risk, w/ knowledge that God will provide the way.

2. What are some other words that communicate the meaning of "empowerment"?

   initiative, solve problems, authority, increasing faith + strength

STUDYING GOD'S WORD

3. In the case of Elijah and Elisha, who initiated the mentoring relationship (see 1 Kings 19:16)?

   God said to Elijah annoint Elisha to succeed you as prophet

4. Read 1 Kings 19:21 and 2 Kings 2:9. In the light of these passages and the information in this chapter, what characteristics of Elisha made him an effective protégé?

   Provided for people by killing his means to return as farmer - gave up his old way of life asked for a double portion of Elijah's spirit.

5. How did the Apostle Paul empower Titus' ministry? (Consider Titus 1:4; 2 Corinthians 2:13; 7:13-15 and 8:23.)

   Called him his son in faith Felt peace of mind when he finds his brother Titus complete confidence, refreshed - a proven tool for the Lord. Heir to Christ

6. List the qualities of a mentor found in Titus 2:6-8.

self-control, set example, doing good, show integrity in teaching, seriousness, soundness of speech.

APPLYING GOD'S WORD

7. How could you apply the principles of mentoring that are taught in Titus 2:6-8?

In all conversations show patience & integrity, let your words be true & sound.

KEY VERSE:

Meditate on and memorize 2 Kings 2:9.

Let me inherit a double portion of your spirit.

CHAPTER TWELVE

Friendship Can Become Mentoring

Mentoring generally refers to the relationship between an older and younger person. A mentor may be only a few years down the road of life from his protégé. A college student can mentor a high school student. Someone in their twenties can coach the college student. A parent of teens can teach by example a parent with younger children. A couple married for a decade can model for newlyweds. Empty nesters can mentor a couple with teens. A senior saint can guide a man in mid-life. Typically, the older, more experienced person mentors the less experienced person.

However, in the constellation of mentoring relationships, sometimes peers mentor one another. Stanley and Clinton call some friendships "peer co-mentoring." Co-mentoring wouldn't characterize every friendship but some relationships have a closeness to inspire and a candidness to provide accountability. These are friendships with intentionality.

In peer co-mentoring each friend brings different strengths to the relationship. A friend may have skill in one area. The other friend reciprocates with greater strengths in other dimensions of life. I appreciate the co-mentoring of other pastors and colleagues in ministry. They have and continue to come alongside to encourage and exhort me to be the man of God I should be.

Jonathan and David

Stanley and Clinton identify Jonathan and David of the Scriptures as co-mentors.

> Jonathan and David were about the same age, young leaders with great futures. Under normal circumstances, one would expect that they would be competitors and resent one another, but the opposite was true. Unlike Jesus' disciples, who seemed to always vie for the best place and elbow one another in the process, David and Jonathan constantly sought each other's best (1 Samuel 20)— even at the risk of their own lives.[84]

Jonathan was King Saul's son, possible heir to the throne of Israel. Saul perceived David to be a great threat (see 1 Sam. 18:8-9). However, in reality David was a greater threat to Jonathan's position, power, and future.

Jonathan was a great soldier (see 1 Sam. 13:3; 14:1,13-14). He trusted God's help in battle. Saul's son was a person of strength and character. He was willing to address injustice squarely, even if it meant challenging his father or risking his own security (for example, 1 Sam. 14:29-30). And, most importantly, he was a genuine friend to David.

A Co-mentor Cares About His Friend

A co-mentoring friendship requires sacrificial love. This friend is as concerned for the well-being of the other person as he is for himself (see 1 Sam. 20:17). Friendship is a pledge of mutual loyalty. Jonathan and David expressed that commitment of co-mentors. "Jonathan made a covenant with David because he loved him as himself" (1 Sam. 18:3a). This special friendship endured even when it became clear that David was to replace Jonathan as successor to his father's throne.

A Co-mentor Trusts His Friend

Co-mentoring is based on respect, admiration, and trust. Jonathan was drawn to a friendship with David because he was trusting in the Lord and he admired that trust (1 Sam. 19:5). He also admired David's courage and commitment. A co-mentoring friendship is rooted in mutual faith. Stanley and Clinton conclude:

> A final ingredient necessary to the dynamics of co-mentoring centers around openness, trust, commitment, confidentiality. . . . So then, words like acceptance, chemistry, fun, time together, openness, trust, confidentiality, and commitment describe the ingredients of an effective relationship that co-mentors should seek.[85]

A peer mentor knows his friend's motives and comes to his defense even when he is misrepresented by others. A true friend supports his buddy in the other's presence or absence (see 1 Sam. 19:4). A friend seeks reconciliation on behalf of his co-mentor (1 Sam. 19:6-8). A friend protects his brother (1 Sam. 20:12-15). He anticipates problems and helps his friend overcome those obstacles.

A Co-mentor Is Willing to Confront

"Wounds from a friend can be trusted" (Prov. 27:6). Co-mentors will not always agree, but will address issues of disagreement honestly. One afternoon a member of my congregation stopped into my office with this peculiar request, "I am having a problem with John. Would you go talk to him. I can't because he's my friend." I responded, "If he really is your friend then you are the best person to talk to him about the problem. You need to go to him."

A friend is available in times of need (1 Sam. 20:4). Fundamental to bonding is availability. True friends have access to one another. This availability must be mutually sought. "A friend loves at all times, and a brother is born for adversity" (Prov. 17:17).

A Co-mentor Shares His Heart

The Lord Jesus modeled friendship toward his disciples: "I no longer call you servants, because a servant does not know his master's business. Instead, I have called you friends, for everything I learned from my Father, I have made known to you" (John 14:15).

A co-mentor shares his heartfelt feelings (1 Sam. 20:10). The closeness of a relationship is found in the transparency of one's inner thoughts and feelings. "The amount of personal information that one person is willing to disclose to another appears to be an index of the 'closeness' of the relationship and of the affection, love, or trust that prevails between the two people."[86] Jonathan shared his heart with David. Men often fail in friendship because they will not become vulnerable by sharing their inner feelings.

Peer Co-mentoring Is Rooted in Mutual Trust

Friendship, like prayer, is based upon trust and speaking the truth to one another. C.S. Lewis once said, "Friends can say anything to one another and be quite sure that no confidence will be broken."[87]

Friendship means risk and exposure of weakness (1 Sam. 23:15-18). Jonathan remained a friend of David all the days of his life. In the end, David deeply grieved the death of his dear co-mentor.

Daniel and His Friends

Perhaps another example of co-mentoring in the Bible is the friendship of Daniel with Hananiah, Mishael and Azariah. They grew up together, went to school together and faced adversity with common resolve (Dan. 1:8-21).

Most importantly they shared an uncompromising faith in the Lord. When Daniel searched for God's revelation, he turned to his friends for counsel and intercession (Dan. 2:17-18). As a mentor Daniel empowered his friends to greater opportunities of leadership (Dan. 2:49).

Summary

Mentors may be friends, but not all friends are mentors. The nature of the relationships of David and Jonathan and Daniel and his friends that raised them to the level of mentoring was that they protected and empowered each other. These friendships deepened character and empowered accomplishment. These friendships blended commitment with accountability. A friendship may be casual but co-mentoring is intentional.

CHAPTER TWELVE REVIEW

DISCUSSING ISSUES

1. Men in America have been characterized as the "friendless male"? Why do many men find it difficult to cultivate friendships?

   They have trouble getting in touch w/ their inner feelings & lack trust when failures are revealed in confidentiality

2. How much older should a mentor be than his protégé to effectively help his protégé? Which is more important—age or experience?

   Usually a few years older is good, except when their spiritual life is being used as a measuring tool.

STUDYING GOD'S WORD

3. What are the outstanding qualities of the friendship of Jonathan and David? (Consider 1 Samuel 18:3; 19:4-8; 20:4, 10, 17; and 23: 15-18.)

   love your friend as yourself
   He recalled David's exploits to Saul & commended him for his deeds.
   Revealing Truth - God reveals in dreams.

4. What would characterize Daniel's friendships as co-mentoring relationships? (Consider Daniel 1:8-21; 2:17-18, 49.)

   Stood by his conviction not to eat defiled food.

APPLYING GOD'S WORD

5. How could you strengthen and intentionalize some of your friendships to become co-mentoring relationships?

   Chose less than many, Wait for the Lord's leading & go from there, don't start your own - do it for Gods' glory.

6. Give some examples of mentors or protégés in your experience?

A Paul who is more experienced and usually older _from older + more sincere_

A Barnabas who like Jonathan and David is a co-mentor _listened to God then moved_

A Timothy who is a less experienced person _was obedient + trust worthy to Paul's teachings_

KEY VERSE:

Memorize and meditate on John 15:15.

Jesus no longer calls his disciples servants, but friends because they know him more intimately.

CHAPTER THIRTEEN

From Parent to Mentor

Parenting and mentoring are different roles. Both are essential relationships for transferring convictions, character, and skills from one generation to the next. However, each is unique. And both are needed.

In April of 2008 I (Dino) accepted the invitation to become the ninth president of Davis College. The initial agreement was that I would continue with the ministry I was a part of in South Florida. My weekly schedule included preaching on Sunday morning in South Florida and then boarding the 4:15pm flight from the Fort Lauderdale/Hollywood airport and fly to Binghamton, New York through Philadelphia. I returned on the early flight out of Binghamton on Wednesday morning. These weekly flights often produced unique conversations. Because of the collection of nearly 400,000 miles of flying I usually had the best seat on the airplane. First class, first row!

On one flight I sat next to a handsome young man. He engaged me in conversation and I found that he was a freshman student at Temple University. He asked me about my work and I told him a few things about our college. Upon finding that our institution was "religious" in nature he then asked me about God and his question was typical. "How do you know there really is a God?" I went to Psalm 19 and began to share a few things with him from that great Psalm. That Psalm begins with the marvelous words, "The heavens declare the glory of God..." I shared with him from the passage that God can be known through the wonders above, the word of God, and through his people. At the end of the conversation I asked him if he would like to accept Jesus Christ into his heart as his Savior? After a moment or two of quiet thought he said, "No". I asked him if I had made it clear and he responded affirmatively but then he said he had a problem. I asked him what it was and he said "I have a great father and he does not believe there is a God and I would have to ask him about accepting Christ!" I gave the young student my business card and requested that his father email me or call me. I have not heard from his father.

In the course of the conversation the student reminded me that his father taught him many things and that they both were very close. His father was obviously a mentor to his son. The father's influence was obvious. Yet I could not escape the fact that his mentoring had led this searching son of his away from God and not to God.

Every man and woman who has Christ in their life can assume there is an influence they have with others. Influence is very powerful. Perhaps we all minimize the power of our influence. It would be wise for all of us to invest our lives in someone who needs it and to recognize that influence is powerful! Influence is the power to affect and alter someone's development. The power of the gospel that teaches the death, burial, and resurrection of Christ is riveting. Coming to him and following him is worth. Someone needs to show the way. That influence is not only in salvation but it is seen in strengthening someone's walk with God.

Contrasting Parenting and Mentoring

The parent-child relationship is parent-directed. Mom and Dad set the perimeters for the child's behavior and development. Parents don't approach a young child and ask, "What are your goals in life?" The parent should not ask, "Johnny, do you want to go to church on Sunday?" Based on the authority of the Word of God and their wisdom in life, parents determine what is best for the child.

The Apostle Paul instructed fathers to bring up their children in "the training and instruction of the Lord" (Eph. 6:4). This is a father-led process under the guidance of God's Word. The child needs to be following his father's directives. Parents need to teach spiritual truths, character responsibilities, physical disciplines, academic skills, and social graces. Parents are helping their children prepare for the tasks of adult life.

Parental goals are sensitive to the distinctive needs and abilities of each child. Solomon counsels, "Train a child in the way he should go, and when he is old he will not turn from it" (Prov. 22:6). Some commentators interpret the expression, "the way he should go," to mean training that ascertains the unique character of each child. The parent shapes the child's direction in a way that is custom-fit to his or her God-given abilities. The expression certainly refers to "the way" of wise living under the counsel of God's Word.

As the child grows, the parent reduces external constraints with a view to the child internalizing convictions. This means less control and more choices as the young adult matures. Approaching the end of high school and beyond, he or she needs to take more responsibility for decisions. The young adult needs to experience the consequences of personal choices.

A father should ask his young adult, "What does the Lord want you to do with your life? What are your goals? How can your mother and I help you reach those goals?" By the time your child is financially independent and living on his own, the parental role should transition from parent to mentor. In contrast to a parent-directed relationship, the mentor stays on the protégé's agenda.

The mentor has a different role. He enters the relationship to encourage and inspire. The relationship is primarily protégé-directed. The mentor tries to discover the protégé's concerns and goals and helps protect, empower, and inspire him toward reaching those targets.

As I (Peter) was growing up, my mom and dad would pray for other Christian models to enter my life . . . especially during the teen years. Historically this role has been filled by uncles and aunts, older cousins and even grandparents. My parents made sure that I was involved in a church that had an active youth ministry.

During Middle School, I had a dynamic youth pastor, Lenny Seidel, who took me under his wings and encouraged me. Lenny, a gifted musician, inspired four young men in the church to use music skills in ministry— three trumpeters and one pianist. He gathered us together, rehearsed us and gave us opportunities to perform in church. I remember the first musical arrangement Lenny gave us to practice. He admonished us to rehearse diligently because when we performed it we would not be using the score! Play by heart? I was terrified!

Under Lenny's tutelage we developed a music ministry called "Trumpeters for Christ." We enjoyed traveling throughout the New England States. Although we didn't compete with the current popular brass group, Chicago, we sure enjoyed using our limited talents in ministry. Three of the members of Trumpeters for Christ are active in Christian ministry today. In part, that was because we became active in church ministry while we were teens.

Parents Become Mentors

Ideally as the child matures and enters adulthood, the parents' role changes. When young people grow up, leave home, and secure their own financial support, they must be treated as adults. As adults they are now responsible for their own decisions and the consequences of those decisions. Parental control is not only inappropriate but, in most cases, impossible.

A healthy transition can take place in the relationship. The parent should function more as a mentor. From a parent-directed role there should be a transition to a protégé-initiated agenda.

When I (Peter) was coming to the conclusion of my years at Wheaton College I was wrestling with the question of a life vocation. I had been admitted to a graduate program at Fuller School of Psychology and was contemplating working as a clinical psychologist. On the other hand, I had long felt the tug to pastoral ministry.

I spent time alone with the Lord fasting and praying for days. I wrestled with the two alternatives. Should I be a pastor or a psychologist? I considered both directions to be opportunities to serve the Lord. But what was God's will? I felt like I was positioned at Robert Frost's poetic "two roads" that "diverged in a yellow wood."

I called my dad to ask for his guidance. I described my dilemma and my reasons for considering both options. I told him how exceptional the opportunity was to be accepted into the psychology program. After my extended monologue, dad's response was brief, "I have absolute confidence, Peter, that whatever decision you make will be the right one and I will support you in your decision. I love you and I am proud of you." My father's affirmation and respect propelled me into manhood, but he didn't give me the answer to my question.

Since, Fuller's program included a master's degree in theology and Wheaton College Graduate School offered a similar program, I asked for a one-year deferment in my admission. I enrolled in Wheaton's program and postponed my decision.

In my first semester of Wheaton's graduate school I plunged into New Testament studies. After only a few weeks I recognized that my first love was for the study of the Bible and I could still help hurting people through pastoral counseling. I decided to head on to seminary after completing my M.A. at Wheaton. My dad, who had set the course for my life as a young person, made the transition to mentor rather than parent as he helped me through one of life's complex decisions.

What Mentors and Parents Share in Common

Many of the qualities of a parenting relationship should also be true of the mentoring relationship. Modeling, commitment, and self-sacrifice are true of both parent and mentor.

Deuteronomy 6:1-9 describes the character of a father but also of a mentor. Moses was concerned for the future generations of Israelites. He wanted them to experience God's abundance in the promised land.

The context for Deuteronomy 6 is that Moses was giving his parting message to the people of Israel from the area beyond the Jordan. The people were about to enter into the promised land to take possession of it and to live in it. In this message Moses reiterated God's past blessings upon His people and God's commandments for His people. Moses described the kind of spiritual leadership needed for transferring spiritual truth to the next generation.

I have been impressed by four guidelines for spiritual leadership from this passage of Scripture. Although these guidelines are addressed to fathers, the truths are particularly applicable to mentors as well.

Guideline One: Establish your *priorities* by *loving* the Lord above all (Deut. 6:4-5).

Guideline Two: Know your *principles* by *learning* God's Word personally (6:6).

Guideline Three: Share your *presence* by *lending* time to the next generation (6:7).

Guideline Four: Put your priorities and principles into *practice* by *living* out your convictions (6:8-9 and also 1-3).

Guideline One: Establish your *priorities* by *loving* the Lord above all (Deut. 6:4-5). Effective transfer of spiritual truth to others begins with having the right priorities in our own lives. "Hear, O Israel; the Lord our God, the Lord is one" (Deut. 6:4, NASB). The verse begins what constitutes the *shema*. That word is the Hebrew imperative, "Hear!" The *shema* is Judaism's great confession of faith. Two times each day pious Jews recite this portion of Scripture. This verse of Scripture affirms the uniqueness of God. He alone is God.

Moses declared that because God is the only God, He deserved whole-hearted commitment. "Love the Lord your God with all your heart and with all your soul and with all your strength" (Deut. 6:5). The Lord is worthy of our highest affection and complete devotion.

God doesn't want mere observance of external rituals such as reading Scripture, attending church, being baptized, serving on committees and giving tithes. He is concerned about more than following a list of do's and don'ts. That is mere legalism. We are familiar with the Pharisees who were known for their careful observance of external rituals.

God wants us to love Him. The spiritual leader's love should be with the heart, soul, and strength. In Hebrew psychology, the heart is the center of the volition and intellect as well as the emotions. The heart (*labab*) is where decisions are made. The Hebrews didn't have a "head" versus "heart" dichotomy. They spoke of feelings emerging from the intestines! The soul (*nephesh*) refers to the life of the person. According to Genesis 2:24, "The Lord formed the man from the dust of the ground and breathed into his nostrils the breath of life, and the man became a living being" (literally, "soul" *nephesh*). The soul consists of the whole person, physical and spiritual. The "soul" is also used in reference to the spiritual dimension of the person who is in pursuit of God (Psalm 42:1-2 and 103:1-2). The strength (*machad*) focuses on the physical might of a person. It may also speak of loving God with intensity and force.

One way of interpreting this passage is to think of a man loving God with three different parts of his being—the volitional, spiritual and physical dimensions. Another viewpoint is that each word—heart, soul and strength—is a reference to the whole person from a different perspective. The repetition emphasizes the completeness of obedience and commitment. That is, because the Lord alone is God we should love Him completely, wholly, and unreservedly!

Whatever we invest our whole heart, soul and strength into is our "god." If money is your god, then your children will know it and seek to attain it. If pleasure is your god, your children will learn to follow your example. If "churchianity" is your god, your kids will detect it and detest it. If work is your god, your children will be neglected. What would our children say is most important to us?

The Lord must be our number one priority if we are going to effectively pass the spiritual baton on to the next generation. If we are to transmit spiritual truths to our children or protégés we must establish spiritual priorities in our own lives. When the Lord is in his appropriate, central place then everything else will be in the right perspective.

A mentor is concerned with the development of the whole person. A mentor should model that wholeness. That is true integrity. We learn from this Scripture that an ideal mentor is one who loves the Lord. You should seek a mentor who is a believer and is living out his or her faith. The Psalmist reminds us, "Blessed is the man who does not walk in the counsel of the wicked . . ." (Psalm 1:1a). An ungodly mentor may corrupt your life like a computer virus.

Guideline Two: Know your *principles* by *learning* God's Word personally (Deut. 6:6). God's Word is to be "known by heart." We need to be reading, listening to, meditating upon, and memorizing God's Word. When my work required traveling long distances by car, I found that listening to the Scriptures read was helpful. Then when we are faced with a decision, a problem, a question or an opportunity to witness, God's Spirit can direct our thoughts to His Word and apply it to the situation we are facing. Have you found that a Bible is not handy when you are facing the toughest questions. The kids especially like to ask hard questions when you are driving!

If we are to communicate effectively with the younger generation we cannot simply appeal to personal preference ("As long as you are living under my roof!") or tradition ("That's the way it has always been done!"). Instead, we must base our instruction on God's Word and show how we have found it to be true in our life experience.

Guideline Three: Share your *presence* by *lending* time to the next generation (Deut. 6:7). "Impress them [these commandments] on your children. Talk about them when you sit at home and when you walk along the road and when you get up." Learning is most effective in the context of everyday living not in the sterile environment of a classroom. Values are more often caught than taught. They are transmitted through the routine interaction of a day. Many fathers travel to their work. Yet, our young people need both quality and quantity of time.

The Scripture challenges us to "impress" the truths on our children. The Hebrew verb root is *shanan* that literally means to sharpen like the sharpness of an arrow so that the truth penetrates the target. How can a spiritual leader sharpen the teaching of God's Word so that it penetrates the heart of a younger person? First, we communicate God's truth with sharpness when we spend time with a person so that truth is taught in the context of real life situations. How about teaching respect for governmental authority while driving the speed limit? Ouch! Second, we teach the Bible with sharpness when the Lord is first in our own lives. A young person can see the truth lived out in practice. Third, sharpness in instruction comes when we know God's Word and can apply it to each situation. And fourth, perhaps most importantly, truth penetrates the heart when it is presented with love! A young person listens to a man who cares about him and accepts him.

The most important principle of this passage is that we need to spend time with young people if we are going to effectively transfer spiritual truth to them. This means formal times as well as informal times— working together, serving together, and having fun together.

What keeps us from giving time? Many cite the pressure of job expectations. The high-tech world and global economy have increased time demands on the job. Television is a drain on time for many men. Monday Night Football is a real tug! Television especially hurts quality time because it leads to passivity rather than dialogue.

Share your presence. Lend both a quality and quantity of time to the next generation. If you are going to be an effective mentor, it means a commitment of time. Parents, if you are going to be impacting your children, it means carving out time.

Guideline Four: Put your priorities and principles into *practice* by *living* out your convictions (Deut. 6:1-3 and 8-9). "Tie them as symbols on your hands and bind them on your foreheads. Write them on the doorframes of your houses and on your gates" (Deut. 6:8-9). In later Judaism, the Jews took these verses in a literal, legalistic way. Phylacteries were small receptacles containing these verses of Scripture bound to the forehead and the left arm of an orthodox Jewish man during prayer. Later the Jews placed a copy of these verses in a small metal box or skin bag. They attached it on the front door post of the house—a "mezuzah" meaning a door post.

What was Moses' point? Parents, and in this application mentors, should practice God's commands in their daily lives. "On your hand" indicates your actions. "On your forehead" points to your thoughts. "On your door post" refers to daily life in the home. Model your message. Practice what you preach.

Summary

Don't drop the baton! Impact the next generation for Christ as a dad or mom—and as a mentor. Establish your priorities by putting the Lord first. Study God's Word for yourself so that you have a basis for your convictions. Spend a quantity of quality time with your child or protégé. Model your message.

CHAPTER THIRTEEN REVIEW

DISCUSSING ISSUES

1. What is the difference between parenting and mentoring?

   Parenting is influencing our child by your walk w/ God, using more control & less choices until the child matures. Mentoring picks up at the crossroads & eventually gives the lead.

2. Why is it important for parents to make the transition to mentoring?

   After passing the baton w/ God's direction, the mature child is ready to walk alone.

3. What hinders parents from making the transition to mentoring?

   Trust in child & God.

STUDYING GOD'S WORD

4. What are the four guidelines for a mentor and father according to Deuteronomy 6:4-9? Illustrate each of these guidelines from your personal experience.

5. What can a spiritually mature man do to "impress" (literally, "sharpen") the truth of God's Word so that it penetrates the heart of a young man?

APPLYING GOD'S WORD

6. What would our children say we value most in our lives? What areas are keeping you from putting the Lord first in your life?

7. How can you adjust your schedule to have more time for these important relationships?

KEY VERSE:

Meditate on and memorize Deuteronomy 6:7.

CHAPTER FOURTEEN

Say Uncle

Billy, the school bully, was beating me (Peter) up on the elementary school playground. Finally, he put me in a secure headlock and demanded, "Say, Uncle."

I thought to myself, "Is that supposed to humiliate me? I like my uncles." So I said, "Uncle."

Billy did not release me. I had submitted to his demand too quickly. So he tightened his grip and intensified his demand, "Say, Uncle. . . BILLY!"

My neck was really hurting at this point. I thought his request was reasonable considering the alternative was a broken neck. So I said, "Uncle Billy." Billy released me. He was the undisputed champion of the school playground and I was still alive!

Historically, a significant source of mentors was in your extended family. Uncles, aunts, older cousins and grandparents all served to provide the modeling and mentoring to challenge your view of life, expand your vision of opportunity, and strengthen your character.

Mobility has separated many extended families. While my work has brought my family and me to upstate New York, my children's uncles and aunts have lived in places from Boston to Denver. Is that true of your family as well?

Ron's Uncle Ken

As I was writing this chapter our family was enjoying a weeklong vacation on beautiful Martha's Vineyard off the coast of Cape Cod. It was very gracious of extended family to share their vacation home with us.

It is early in the morning. It is quiet. The birds are singing. This is my favorite time of the day! I am looking out over the Atlantic Ocean and listening to the steady crashing of the waves.

My son, Ron, has recently completed his driver education class and passed his driver's test for a full license. But, he has only learned to drive cars with automatic transmissions. Uncle Ken ferried over a car with a standard transmission. How many of you would share your car with a young driver?

Ken showed Ron how to drive with the stick shift. Then he went out driving with his nephew. Ron stalled a few times, squeaked the wheels and ground the gears, but he was a quick understudy. Then, in an act of courage or craziness, Ken gave him the keys to his car and said, "Take it for a spin!" Ron was off. He was back a few hours later with a new level of capability and confidence. He had a great time! Mentors expand opportunities and encourage effort.

Uncle Ken trusted Ron, instructed him, modeled for him and released him to drive the car himself. Those are characteristics of mentoring!

Esther's Uncle Mordecai

In the book of Esther, God sovereignly intervened to protect the Jewish people. They were living in exile under the reign of the Persian monarch Xerxes. God's sovereignty is evident through the dismissal of Xerxes' queen, the elevation of Esther to that regal position, Mordecai's discovery of a plot against the king, and the miraculous deliverance of the Jewish people from Haman's wicked plot.

The biblical story of Esther also illustrates mentoring by an extended family member. "Mordecai had a cousin named Hadassah, whom he had brought up because she had neither father or mother. This girl who was also known as Esther, was lovely in form and features, and Mordecai had taken her as his own daughter when her father and mother died" (Esth. 2:7).

Mordecai was an adoptive parent who transitioned to become a mentor for his younger "cousin" Esther (Esth. 2:7, literally, "his uncle's daughter"). Rabbinic tradition, as well as the Jewish historian Josephus, identify Esther as Mordecai's niece.

A Relationship of Trust

In the absence of Esther's parents, Mordecai cared for her and brought her up (*'omen*). The Hebrew word, *'omen*, translated "brought up" means to confirm and support. It is the same word from which "Amen" is derived. The word is used in reference to the strong arms of a mother holding her infant. The word is also used of pillars supporting a building.

Mordecai's nurturing built a strong foundation for Esther's life. He established her security and wellbeing. He showed confidence in her. Esther trusted her "uncle." That trust formed the foundation of the mentoring relationship.

"Esther had not revealed her nationality and family background, because Mordecai had forbidden her to do so" (Esther 2:10). She continued to follow her mentor's instruction as she had done when he was bringing her up (Esther 2:19-20). Esther demonstrated her complete trust in Mordecai by following his counsel. From the time she first came under his care, she had listened to him and submitted to his guidance. This continued even after she was elevated to the position of queen.

A Mentor Cares for His Protégé

Mordecai demonstrated genuine concern for the wellbeing of his protégé. According to Esther 2:11, "Every day he walked back and forth near the courtyard of the harem to find out how Esther was and what was happening to her." Mordecai's effort to be in contact with Esther demonstrated care, perseverance, and cleverness. He wanted to protect her interests and to provide advice for her effectiveness.

A Mentor Empowers His Protégé

Following Haman's plot against the Jewish people, Mordecai urged Esther to go into the king's presence to beg for mercy and to plead with him for her people (Esther 4:8). Esther did not defy Mordecai's command. However, she thought compliance was impossible (Esther 4:10-11).

As a mentor, Mordecai empowered his protégé for action in three ways. First, he modeled courage and faith when he refused to bow in idolatry (Esther 3:2). Second, he explained to Esther her possible courses of action and the consequences of such action (Esther 4:12-17). And ultimately, Mordecai directed Esther to understand and submit to the providence of God: "Who knows but that you have come to royal position for such a time as this?" (Esther 4:14). Thus, Mordecai empowered Esther for action enabling her to risk her life for the endangered Jewish people.

There were two levels of mentoring in Mordecai's relationship with Esther. First, as a mentor, Mordecai provided a framework for values that connected her with the past and the future. Mordecai helped Esther to remember her spiritual heritage and to recognize her God-given power.

Second, as an effective mentor, Mordecai helped Esther to develop in two different cultures—the Persian court and the Hebrew community. He was an ideal mentor because he gave Esther a larger context for her life than the king's culture. Mordecai helped her identify her strengths, and yet gave her a basic sense of values that went beyond her appearance. The spiritual heritage which Mordecai gave to Esther freed her from bondage to the cultural constraints on women.[9]

Summary

Uncles and Aunts have a special opportunity to model life for their nephews and nieces. Mordecai demonstrated that significant influence in Esther's life. My son Ron has watched me work in various full-time Christian ministries throughout his life. That would limit his perspective on life's opportunities if he wasn't exposed to others. I know Ron appreciated his youth pastors— Joel, Keith, Andrew, Wes and Ken. They modeled, listened, taught and encouraged him. Availability has been a key to their effectiveness. Also, there have been teachers at school, men in the church, neighbors and friends who have made an impact. But, uncles have a special place in his life and experience.

Ron's uncles demonstrate how to live for God in different callings. On our way to Martha's Vineyard we visited Uncle Scott. He is an accountant in a multinational corporation. He also is active in leadership in the church. He led the worship service at his church where we attended on Sunday. He showed a layman's involvement in ministry. Scott has made tough decisions to balance the demands of corporate culture and the priorities of family and church.

Ron's Uncle Preston is a Harvard Medical School professor and research scientist. Ron is inspired by his work and his example. Preston is integrating his Christian faith into the medical world. Ron worked as the IT\marketing guy for his Uncle Phil in the ServiceMaster industry and learned about the challenges of being a small business owner.

Like Mordecai, Ron's uncles are demonstrating how to live in two different cultures—the Christian community and the world of business and medicine. Today, Ron is a Christian businessman marked by integrity. He is successful in the marketplace, but more importantly, he is a faithful husband, dedicated father, and a committed participant in his church.

CHAPTER FOURTEEN REVIEW

DISCUSSING ISSUES

1   Describe a significant uncle, older cousin or grandfather who has made a positive influence in your life.

2.   Consider the example of Uncle Ken teaching Ron to drive. How does that example illustrate mentoring?

STUDYING GOD'S WORD

3.   What are the key qualities of Mordecai's effectiveness as a mentor to his younger cousin or niece? (Consider Esther 2:7, 10-11, 19-20; 3:2; 4:8, and 10-17.)

4.   How did Mordecai empower Esther for expanded ministry (see Esther 4:8-17)?

5.   What qualities of an effective protégé are demonstrated by Esther?

APPLYING GOD'S WORD

6. Where does your extended family live? How could you help mentor your nephews who live nearby? How could you mentor your family members who live at a distance?

KEY SCRIPTURE

Meditate on and memorize Proverbs 27:17.

Part 3
Getting Started

CHAPTER FIFTEEN

Mentoring Takes Aim

Perhaps more than any other ministry to men and boys, in my (Peter's) life Christian Service Brigade (CSB) captures the essence of mentoring. Understanding that "boys will be men," it is committed not only to instruct but also to equip young men to become leaders. The leaders of CSB do that by modeling for the boys and then delegating responsibility to them.

I can still remember the leaders who invested in my life as a "Stockader." We built crafts, played games, listened to stories about adventures in lives of Christian men, went on camping trips, memorized Scripture, and explored the Frontier Camp.

CSB is built on the principle of giving leadership authority to young men. These young men will be effective leaders later if they are entrusted with authority now. The core of the program is mentoring. Men invest time in younger men who invest time in boys. This time is not only spent in learning spiritual disciplines but also in developing physical skills and sharing adventures in life like camping.

When my son, Ron, was eight, we headed to the Adirondacks of New York State for a long weekend of father and son camping at Northern Frontier Christian Service Brigade Camp. We soaked in the outdoor setting— fishing, catching frogs, hiking, sailing and swimming. Ron especially looked forward to the rifle and archery ranges.

At the archery range, Ron learned how to use a bow and arrow for the first time. Together with other young archers, the arrows began to fly, but few even hit the target. Some arrows sailed over, some veered sideways, many fell short and one even went backwards! Some of the boys became frustrated and discouraged. When the supervisor announced that it was the last arrow, Ron pulled his arrow back slowly, then released. Whoosh. Thud. Bull's eye! Together, we shared the thrill of accomplishment!

Similarly, mentoring must aim at a target. What kind of person is qualified to be a mentor? What is the goal of the protégé who enters a mentoring relationship? As Christ-followers we must aim at the target of spiritual maturity. The Apostle Paul provided one of the most detailed descriptions of that target. He described the qualities for spiritual leadership in his letters to Timothy and Titus. In 1 Timothy, chapter three, he identified those targets as qualifications of an "overseer" or "bishop" (*episkopos*). In Titus, chapter one, we find the parallel leadership prerequisites for an "elder" (*presbuteros*) and "overseer" (*episkopos*). In Titus 2, Paul describes the qualities of a mature woman who can teach younger women.

Paul's overarching word to summarize the qualities of a competent, spiritually mature leader is *anepilemptos* translated "above reproach" (1 Tim. 3:2, NIV). The term means "faultless and irreproachable."[88] The Greek word literally means "not to be laid hold of." That is, it is impossible to bring any charge of wrongdoing against this godly man because of his integrity and character.[89] The spiritual leader is one who has a good reputation and deserves it. This is the spiritual bull's eye for both mentor and protégé.

The expression, "above reproach", summarizes the following five targets of a spiritual leader: (1) he serves the church body, (2) he communicates spiritual truth, (3) he becomes Christlike in personal maturity, (4) he leads effectively in the home, and (5) he demonstrates integrity outside the church. These five qualities of spiritual leadership are the personal targets for the protégé in a mentoring relationship. He takes aim with his arrows for the targets of church involvement, biblical communication, a Christlike personal walk, a godly home life and integrity in the community.

Aim to Serve the Church Family

The first target described by Paul is that a man "aspire to" or "set his heart on" serving the spiritual needs of others in the local body of believers (1 Tim. 3:1). The verb, *oregetai*, translated "sets his heart on," literally means "to stretch oneself, reach out one's hand."[90]

The Apostle Paul is not commending striving for position and power. Aspiring for a title is wrong; seeking to serve others is godly. "One needs to be sure that such a desire is not an expression of carnal pride, but rather that it reflects a deep consecration to the work of the church."[91] Church leadership is service to others, not acquisition for oneself. An "overseer" watches over the needs of the believers in the local body.

Paul is primarily commending the "noble task," not the aspiration itself. The task of spiritual leadership is a good work. "Paul is not commending people who have a great desire to become leaders; rather, he is saying that the position of church leader is such a significant matter, an excellent work, that it should indeed be the kind of task to which a person might aspire."[92]

The aspiration is also commended because it involves cultivating godly qualities of character. One who aspires for spiritual leadership seeks to develop Christlike character in his own life.

Therefore, the first target of the mentor and protégé is twofold: to cultivate godly character and to care for the spiritual needs of the body of believers. This genuine concern for the wellbeing and empowering of others is essential to the effective mentor.

There is a declining interest in spiritual leadership in the church. Both lay leaders and pastoral leaders are increasingly difficult to find. They are under appreciated and under attack. As a result, Leith Anderson anticipates that we will be facing a dearth of pastoral leaders in the coming years.[93] Paul is saying it is a good thing to desire to serve the body of Christ by developing the godly character of an overseer in the church.

Aim to Know and to Teach God's Word

> The finest and most effective teaching is done not by speaking but by being.

A second target of spiritual leadership is to be "able to teach" (1 Tim. 3:2b). The leader must know God's Word and be able to pass on those biblical truths in an understandable way to others. This does not require the leader to be a gifted public speaker. That communication may take place one-on-one or in a small group rather than from a pulpit.

Effective teaching of spiritual truth requires modeling those truths in daily life. In Titus 1:9, the Apostle Paul listed the ability to teach sound doctrine last in the qualifications for a spiritual leader. This does not diminish the importance of teaching. But it indicates that character must precede communication.

Receptivity to a man's teaching is built upon respect for his character and competence.[94] Crucial to effective communication of spiritual truth is that the teacher models those truths in daily life. "The finest and most effective teaching is done not by speaking but by being. Even the man with no gift of words can teach, by living in such a way that in him men see the reflection of the Master."[95]

Aim for Christlikeness in One's Personal Life

Therefore, a third target of spiritual leadership is Christlike maturity in one's personal life. The Apostle Paul listed a number of personal qualities beginning with "above reproach" (1 Tim. 3:2). This comprehensive term includes all the qualities that follow. "Temperate" (*nephalion*) refers to a man who is not subject to excesses. This not only includes excessive eating and drinking, but excesses in any area of life. Couldn't that term apply today to excesses in watching television, surfing the web, playing sports and even work?[96]

"Self-controlled" (*sophronas*) means to be sensible and reasonable even in one's assessment of self.[97] "Respectable" (*kosmion*) means inward moral excellence expressed in outward orderly behavior.[98] Is your life in order or disarray? Is it marked by moral excellence or compromise?

"Hospitable" (*philoxzenon*) means literally to be a "lover of strangers." This is the quality of reaching out and ministering to those in need. Are you self-absorbed or alert to the needs of people around you? Are you sensitive and responsive, particularly to those who cannot reciprocate your expression of kindness?[99]

The list of personal character qualifications continue. The qualities describe a man who is yielded to the control of the Holy Spirit (e.g., not given to much wine, not violent, gentle, and not quarrelsome). The accumulation of earthly treasure is far from his goal in life (i.e., not a lover of money and not pursuing dishonest gain). Are you uncompromising with respect to the truth of God's Word, but yielding when it comes to your own rights and preferences? Are you angered by moral wrongs or personal inconveniences?

Aim for a Godly Family Life

The fourth target of a spiritual leader is effective management within the home. He is faithful to his wife as literally "a one woman man" (*mias gunaikos andra*, 1 Tim. 3:2). Although this is a reference to his current marital relationship, it may also have implications concerning any past marital commitments. The best thing a man can do for his children is to faithfully love their mother!

With firm, loving, and patient discipline, a spiritual leader ensures that his children are obedient (1 Tim. 3:4). The children are "believers" in the sense of being trustworthy as they live within their parent's guidelines (Titus 1:6). A dad cannot guarantee that his children will be "born from above." He can ensure that they are guided toward the things of God while they are under his supervision. The Apostle asked rhetorically, "If anyone does not know how to manage his own family, how can he take care of God's church?" (1 Tim. 3:5). A fundamental qualification for spiritual leadership in the church is a man's competence in providing for the spiritual, emotional, and physical needs of his family.

Aim for a Good Reputation in the Community

A fifth target of spiritual leadership is a good reputation in the community. This includes integrity and excellence in the workplace, neighborhood, and recreation place. If a spiritual leader is to be trustworthy, he must demonstrate a consistency between his life within the body of believers and his life among the wider community of unbelievers. A man who is to serve in leadership in the church is, for example, to be honest in financial matters (see Titus 1:7). How about paying those taxes when others hide it "off the books"? He must be just in dealing with people, fulfilling his commitments (see "upright" in Titus 1:8). His neighbors will speak well of him.

When the five targets for spiritual leadership are combined, they describe a man who is "above reproach." These qualifications of an elder and overseer are, in fact, the characteristics of an effective mentor. Such qualities are foundational to building a relationship of trust with a protégé. These qualities must also be the targets of the protégés when entering into a mentoring relationship.

The failure of a mentoring relationship can be due to shortcomings in the character of the mentor. The mentor must pursue the qualities delineated by the Apostle Paul, if he is to be trusted and emulated by his protégé in a mentoring relationship.

Nevertheless, all mentors fall short of the target. The Apostle John declares, "If we claim to be without sin, we deceive ourselves and the truth is not in us" (I John 1:8). When a mentor sins, he admits it and then proceeds to correct it. He can be an example to his protégé in both his successes and his failures by how he responds to his shortcomings. When a mentor is vulnerable even concerning his failures, then a protégé learns to address his own failures.

Target Learning Agreements Help Focus the Objectives

There are several reasons for using written learning agreements in a mentoring relationship. I call them "Target Learning Agreements." First, learning agreements provide a vehicle for identifying and clarifying targets for the mentoring process. "The mentor should summarize agreements as he reaches them with his protégé, in order to ensure that there is complete understanding of what has been discussed and what plans have been made."[100]

Second, identifying the target is an important aspect of the learning agreement. Each time the mentoring pair gets together, they should identify short and long-term targets or goals. The goals established should be achievable, realistic, measurable in terms of quality and quantity, and agreed upon between mentor and protégé.[101] Targets help provide direction for the mentoring.

Because mentoring relationships need a balance of freedom and structure, learning agreements must be personalized. This balances the fine line between too much structure and not enough structure.

Third, the learning agreements not only provide accountability for the protégé, they also provide a cooperative task which give the participants a focus and motivation for their mentoring relationship. The agreements can become the "common pursuit" that provide the glue for the relationship to bond.

Summary

If you want to be an effective mentor, take aim at the spiritual targets described by the Apostle Paul. If you want to be a protégé, look for a man who is seeking to be "above reproach." You want to hang around that kind of man and let his "good stuff" rub off on you.

If you "aim at nothing— you will always hit it." But, if you aim the arrows of your life at Christ-like maturity, you will have a lifelong challenge. Go for it! Aim for the bull's eye! Become a man of integrity and character.

CHAPTER FIFTEEN REVIEW

DISCUSSING ISSUES

1. Why are fewer men pursuing leadership responsibilities in the church today?

2. How can we encourage more men to aim toward church leadership?

STUDYING GOD'S WORD

3. Review in your own words the five areas the Apostle Paul targets for a man's personal growth (1Timothy 3 and Titus 1)?

   Target One _____

   Target Two _____

   Target Three _____

   Target Four _____

   Target Five _____

APPLYING GOD'S WORD

4. Discuss the following terms used in the "Target Learning Agreements."

A *need* is an area of your life you believe God wants you to work in.

A *target* is the goal you are aiming for. Select from the five targets mentioned in this chapter.

Learning tasks are specific learning steps. They should be reasonable, measurable.

The *evaluation* concerns how you are doing. Someone should be able to monitor your progress and thus provide accountability.

5. Consider the worksheets on the following pages as a tool to help focus on a target in each of the five dimensions of spiritual maturity. Pick two of the five targets and develop learning agreements in those areas. You can use the samples on the following pages to guide you.

KEY VERSE:

Memorize and meditate on Amos 3:3.

Target Learning Agreement

	SAMPLE #1
PROTÉGÉ	
NEED	
Commitment to serve and participate in the gathering life of the church	
LEARNING TARGET	
To commit myself to attend the corporate meetings of the church for a period of three months	
LEARNING TASKS	
• To attend an Adult Bible Fellowship each week • To attend a worship service each week • To serve in a ministry each week • To participate in a small group each week	
LEARNING EVALUATION	
Register my weekly attendance on a calendar and share with my mentor my observations and suggestions concerning the meetings and ministries	

Target Learning Agreement

MENTOR	SAMPLE #2
PROTÉGÉ	
NEED	
Loving and effective leadership in the home is essential to spiritual leadership in the church	
LEARNING TARGET	
To develop a positive communication pattern with my wife	
LEARNING TASKS	
• To spend one hour of uninterrupted and undistracted time talking with my wife each week • To have a weekly date with my wife for the next three months	
LEARNING EVALUATION	
Ask my wife for a note reflecting her feelings about this time together as a couple	

Target Learning Agreement

MENTOR	
PROTÉGÉ	
NEED	
LEARNING TARGET	
LEARNING TASKS	
LEARNING EVALUATION	

Target Learning Agreement

MENTOR	
PROTÉGÉ	
NEED	
LEARNING TARGET	
LEARNING TASKS	
LEARNING EVALUATION	

CHAPTER SIXTEEN

Mastering Mentoring

Where does the rubber meet the road concerning mentoring? How do you apply the principles of mentoring in your daily life? Mentoring begins with a commitment to invest in the lives of others. The goal of life is not simply to complete the tasks yourself but to multiply work and ministry through others.

Recently I (Dino) presented a lecture to over two hundred pastors and Christian workers on the subject of pastors mentoring the next generation. I personally spoke to several veteran pastors prior to this event who have expressed interest in mentoring and they have shared a concern about their ability to mentor. Their concern is a very real issue. How does one go about finding a mentor is a concern but the greater issue is how does one mentor?

At the presentation I interviewed Christian leaders who have a story to tell. The interviews included my colleague, Peter Mason, who shared great information into mentoring. This book is a gold mine of his insights! Duke Hargett, Matt Euchus, and shared their thoughts on an incredible exchange of the pastors roles. Duke, the senior pastor, handed the lead pastor role to a man nearly (Matt) half his age and became the missions' pastor. Duke's style is very relational and Matt is a strong leader. Both have excellent speaking abilities. The church grew another 150 after the move was made. Mentoring was the key to the change.

Bill Berkheiser pastors a church in the Greater Binghamton community and this graduate of our college does some adjunct teaching for Davis. He has come and looked and picked potential leaders and spends hours with them in a mentorship role which includes everything from visitation to critiquing their messages preached from his pulpit!

Mike Sanders pastors one of America's great churches, The Open Door Church, Chambersburg, Pa. This is a church where I spent 25 years at as the Senior Pastor. Mike is gracious in listing me as one of his mentors and explained to the delegates that as a board member of our college he had to lead the evaluation of his mentor – Me!!

Jack Delaney, of Williamsport, PA. told his story of two attempts to mentor the next pastor of churches he pastored. One was a failure and the second was a success. Often in the mentoring process there are some bumps along the road.

Sitting in the audience was John. John is a student at Davis College who has been saved for two years. Shortly after the meeting John came into my office and bluntly asked, "Will you mentor me?" John is a young man with a heart for God. He and his wife have two children and they are looking forward to the day when John will be a pastor. When someone asks to be mentored it does not necessarily mean that they should be mentored by the person they are requesting. I asked John "What do you want out of the mentoring relationship?" One of the things he said was, "I want this to be long term!" The conference met a goal in that a young man immediately saw the need for mentorship! I recently took John and his wife along to eat with my wife and me. It was sweet fellowship. I look forward to having a part in his life.

Also sitting in the audience was another man named Sal. Sal and I recently roomed together on one of my Israel trips. Sal is between ministries and is working on his master's degree. I asked Sal if he wanted me to mentor him. As I look at him I see myself twenty years ago! Enthusiastic, aggressive, and energy are spilling out all over. I believe he will be greatly used by God. He agreed and I look forward to whatever input I can have in his life.

Here are two men. One rather new in the faith and relatively quiet. The other ready to jump at a moment's notice. Both of these men will be in process with me. The conference set the stage for many other stories of those who are being mentored. My question to them is the same. "What is God doing in your life and where is he at work?" It is not my responsibility to tell them what to do but to guide them in what God is leading them to do in their life. If the 200 plus pastors and Christian leaders who attended the conference would either get into a mentoring role or a mentored role I believe that effective ministry would begin to take place that would multiply itself for the kingdom's sake.

Sals and Johns are everywhere. Jonathan, Adam, Nathanael, JoAnna, Terry, Brad, Kyle, Charles, Bernard, Jack, Marc, Mike, Jerry, Paul, Ben, Jerome, David, Jeff ... These are some of the many names!

They are unique and special individuals. They have a marvelous opportunity for kingdom work. They are in your church, your neighborhoods, and universities. Your time with them is special! The conference at Davis College wets the appetite. The work is now about to begin. Make it enjoyable. Chats over coffee, an occasional meal, phone calls, and other connections will set the stage for time that is well spent!

Levels of Mentoring

Stanley and Clinton identify three levels of mentors: (1) upward mentors, who have gone before and can show the way; (2) downward protégés, who shake our complacency, renew our convictions, keep us on our toes, and multiply our ministry for Christ's kingdom; and (3) peer co-mentors, who know us, identify with us, and provide mutual encouragement and personal accountability.[102] You should pursue involvement in all three levels of mentoring.

Structures of Mentoring

We can apply the upward, downward and peer mentoring relationships in three structures. The first, and most frequent, structure of mentoring is informal. Most mentoring is informal. These are casual friendships between two people who enjoy being with one another and encourage each other. These relationships involve camaraderie and correction.

The second structure of mentoring is intentional. Intentional mentoring often emerges out of casual personal contacts. The participants initiate this mentoring themselves. It is a formalizing of the relationships that increases the accountability and expands the access the participants give to one another. An intentional mentoring relationship agrees to a mutual commitment.

The third structure of mentoring is facilitated mentoring. Facilitated mentoring has an external catalyst to the relationship. A third party designs and organizes the overall structure. At the same time, a facilitated mentoring program builds in opportunities for the participants to make choices. The primary purpose of this kind of mentoring is to systematically develop the character and skills of the less experienced members of an organization. That organization may be a business, educational institution, sports team, club, community agency, church, or parachurch ministry.

Of course, there may be a range of variations that include dimensions of informal and formal mentoring. There is a balance between too much structure and lack of structure.

Informal Mentoring

We can enjoy the camaraderie of friends in our everyday circle of contact. In these relationships we admire others, inspire them to press on, and want to see each other excel in life's responsibilities. We learn from our shared experiences.

Intentional Mentoring

Our lives are very busy. To initiate a mentoring relationship with someone who is not in our present circle of relationships can be difficult. A brand-new relationship takes time, effort and coordination to pull it off. It helps to already have some regular contact points.

I would encourage you to intentionalize relationships that are part of your present routine whether it be at work, church, recreation, or with family. Infuse purpose and direction in those relationships through mentoring. Mentoring brings focus, accountability and continuity to the casual relationships you already enjoy. Mentoring maximizes a relationship.

Remember that mentoring is typically "protégé driven." If you are younger and less experienced in life, don't wait for a more experienced man to initiate the relationship with you. It's your move! He will often be honored by your interest in benefiting from his wisdom and experience.

If you are willing to serve as a mentor, ask God to open an opportunity. When you are involved in a ministry or hobby or area of work, invite someone less experienced to join you. Be a good listener to that less experienced man. Let him share his concerns. Show your interest in his aspirations and interests. Express your willingness to give your time and experience to be a resource to help him achieve his life goals and to solve his problems. Follow his agenda rather than imposing your plan. Have the rewarding experience of investing your time and talent into the life of someone closer to the beginning of life's journey.

Facilitated Mentoring

I (Peter) have a wonderful ministry at my church called FaithMoms. Mature women gather each week with younger moms. Each "group leader" or mentor has an assistant who is developing her leadership skills by observing, interacting and also leading the small group. The groups study a book. However, the discussion questions dig into life application. How can I be a more devoted follower of Christ, a loving wife, and an effective parent? A dedicated staff of childcare workers release these mothers to learn from one another under the guidance of a more experienced mom and follower of Christ. The FaithMom coordinators meet with the mentors once each month to resource them in their ministry. This is an example facilitated mentoring.

The character of our individualistic and increasingly mobile culture is that informal relationships, especially between men, do not develop with frequency or depth. Sociologists refer to men in our society as the "friendless male." This need points to the helpfulness of a facilitated mentoring program designed to be a catalyst for relationships between men with a view to teaching God's Word, strengthening character, and developing leaders. A facilitated program can provide a stimulus for initiating those relationships. It has the primary purpose of systematically developing the less experienced members of the organization whether it be a ministry, school or business.

I helped facilitate a mentoring program when pastoring in New Jersey. It was called the Leadership Acquisition Mentoring Program (LAMP). An exceptional strength of the church was its large group of highly involved senior saints. The high level of commitment and time availability of the spiritual leaders was an asset to the effectiveness of the mentoring program. Most of the men enthusiastically agreed to participate. The degree of their commitment to the process had a significant impact on their effectiveness as mentors.

When the spiritual leaders are involved in mentoring it stimulates a "mentor-rich" environment in the church. That is, the leadership participation provides a pattern of training for other church ministries to follow.

The target of LAMP was to develop biblical understanding, godly character and ministry skills in less experienced men in the church. The protégé's goal was not to attain an office in the church. A by-product of the program was to prepare men who would be spiritually qualified to serve as elders and deacons.

Mentoring requires an intensive personal involvement that cannot be forced on the participants. This points to the importance of voluntarism. To encourage a "voluntary" dimension to this facilitated program, each elder nominated three potential protégés. Each nominee was then invited to participate and to submit the names of three elders he would want as his mentor. I then matched the mentor-protégé dyads. The more voluntary involvement and choice on the part of the participants, the more effective the program.

To help with accountability in mentoring, we suggest that you utilize "target learning agreements." Writing down targets is a vehicle for clarifying and listing objectives for the mentoring relationship. When you summarize agreements in writing, you help ensure that there is complete understanding of what has been discussed and what plans have been made.

The targets established for each of the learning agreements should be achievable and realistic in terms of quality and quantity. Targets help provide direction for the mentoring relationship. These agreements not only provide accountability, but they can also become the "common problems" or "shared pursuits" that provide the glue for the relationship to bond. Because mentoring relationships need a balance of freedom and structure, targeted learning experiences must be individualized to each protégé.

> **The tyranny of the urgent in church life will squeeze out time for the important if mentoring is not a priority.**

Prior to inaugurating the church mentoring program, I encouraged participation through a series of sermons about the biblical examples of mentoring. Experienced church leaders have an interest in developing future leaders. They are concerned about the future health of the church.

One of the biggest challenges to a facilitated mentoring program is the competition for time. The tyranny of the urgent in church life squeezes out time for the important if mentoring is not a priority. Investing time in mentoring relationships may require eliminating some less effective programs. This may also mean releasing spiritual leaders to do mentoring by delegating some of their other responsibilities. For mentoring to take place it requires a willing attitude and a high commitment.

The LAMP program began with an orientation meeting. The elder/mentors led small group prayer fellowships within the context of the church. They trained the protégés in the context of those small groups, helping them learn to lead in Bible study and prayer. They also met one-on-one each week for about one hour to share and to pray with their protégés and to encourage their progress in completing the targeted learning agreements.

Time Framework

There is no substitute for time when cultivating a relationship. Within the church mentoring program I developed, the more effective mentoring relationships included informal times of getting together. Researchers in the field of mentoring agree that effective change, as a result of a mentoring relationship, requires a duration of at least nine months.

Richard Tyre suggests three phases in the mentoring relationship beginning with (1) bonding followed by (2) mutuality and leading to the phase of (3) effective change. During the bonding phase the participants get the structure in place and the relationship running smoothly. During this initiation phase there is the establishment of an environment of trust.

In initiating facilitated mentoring programs, ask for a three-month commitment. This period of time allows the participants to evaluate the relationship. Pre-define the ending point of phase one. This allows the participants to end the relationship without offending the other participant. The mentor and protégé may choose to continue only if both are willing and able.

Summary and Conclusion

May the Lord help you to be a mentor, co-mentor and protégé. Be a Paul, a Barnabas and a Timothy. Enjoy informal mentoring but consider pursuing more intentional relationships.

Invest in the next generation of leaders by *sharing your God-given resources as a mentor*. Consider being a mentor to an extended family member. Perhaps through a youth ministry in your church, you could mentor a promising young man or woman. Come alongside a needy young person in your community and be a mentor. Mentor a young person who is just venturing out in your profession. Give the protégé the benefit of the lessons you have learned and the contacts you have made.

Become a co-mentor. Cultivate a friendship into a mentoring relationship. Purpose in your friendship to stimulate growth in Christ through encouragement and accountability.

Become a protégé. Go to a more experienced person that you respect to seek perspective and counsel. Ask questions like: "What advice would you give a younger person today? If you were my age, what would you do differently? What lessons have you learned?" Ask for wisdom to guide you. Learn from this experience.

Perhaps the Lord would use you *to facilitate a mentoring program* in the life of your church, community or business organization. On the kitchen wall of my (Peter's) childhood home in Connecticut, my mother placed a plaque that read, "Only one life t'will soon be past; only what's done for Christ will last." Life is short. People are important. They will live forever. Look for ways to empower the next generation of young people to be effective servants of Jesus Christ. Make a lasting difference!

CHAPTER SIXTEEN REVIEW

DISCUSSING ISSUES

1. What kind of leadership training programs do you have in your church, workplace or community?

2. How could you enhance the mentoring feature of your leadership development program?

STUDYING GOD'S WORD

3. Give some biblical examples of the following mentors:

   Upward mentor_____

   Downward mentor_____

   Co-mentor _____

4. Which mentoring relationships in the Scripture impressed you the most? What did you learn from those examples?

APPLYING GOD'S WORD

5. Identify a young person to mentor . . . Identify a friendship you could strengthen into a co-mentoring relationship. Identify a more experienced person who could be a mentor to you .

6. Consider the following steps for facilitating a leadership development mentoring program:

STEP 1:   The facilitator introduces the biblical principles of mentoring through:
    a. A series of sermons focusing on biblical examples of mentoring;
    b. A Bible study or book study about mentoring; other suggestions?

STEP 2:   Identify a ministry context for mentoring such as Sunday School, small groups, youth ministries, women's group, _____, etc.

STEP 3:   Recruit volunteers who are willing to be mentors and/or protégés. What are some ways you could solicit volunteers?

STEP 4:   Orientation meeting: Help the mentoring participants to understand their commitments in the program. For example:
    a. Communicate the purpose of the program to all the participants;
    b. Agree to participate in the program for 3 months (or 6 months, etc.);
    c. Participate in the ministry (e.g. small group) once a week;
    d. Meet in a one-on-one or accountability group setting once a week;
    e. Introduce the nature of the "Target Learning Agreements;" and
    f. Establish the first meeting time between the mentors and protégés.

STEP 5:   Utilize "Target Learning Agreements" to clarify the learning objectives for the mentoring relationship.

STEP 6:   The facilitator should meet with each mentoring pair at least once in 3 months. What should the facilitator look for in the mentoring relationships to help them improve?

STEP 7:   Conclude with an evaluation meeting to assess the program. The facilitated relationships may continue informally.

ENDNOTES

1. Henry Cloud, *Changes That Heal* (Grand Rapids, Mich.: Zondervan Publishing House, 1992), 48.

2. Agnes K. Missiriam, *The Corporate Connection* (New York: Prentice Hall, 1982), x.

3. Bobb Biehl, *Mentoring: Confidence in Finding a Mentor and Becoming One* (Nashville: Broadman and Hollman Publishers, 1996), 11.

4. Howard Hendricks, "A Mandate for Mentoring," in *Seven Promises of a Promise Keeper* (Colorado Springs, Colo.: Focus on the Family Publishing, 1994), 50.

5. ibid., 12.

6. ibid., 47-48.

7. Homer, *The Odyssey*, trans. by R. Fitzgerald (New York: Anchor/Doubleday Publishers, 1963).

8. Margo Murray and Marna A. Owen, *Beyond the Myths and Magic of Mentoring* (San Francisco: Jossey-Bass Publishers, 1991), 7.

9. Laurent A. Daloz, *Effective Teaching and Mentoring: Realizing the Transformational Power of Adult Learning Experiences* (San Francisco: Jossey-Bass Publishers, 1986), xviii.

10. Bobb Biehl, Mentoring: *Confidence in Finding a Mentor and Becoming One* (Nashville: Broadman and Holman Publishers, 1996), 21.

11. Murray and Owen, xiv.

12. Howard Hendricks and others, *Mentoring: Catching the Passion— Passing It On* (Dallas, Tex: Dallas Theological Seminary Tape Ministry, 1991), tape no. 1.

13. Cloud, 47.

14. ibid., 49.

15. Paul Stanley and Bobby Clinton, *Connecting: The Mentoring Relationships You Need to Succeed in Life* (Colorado Springs, Colo.: Navpress, 1992), 33.

16. John K. Rempel and John G. Holmes, "How Do I Trust Thee?" *Psychology Today* (February 1986), 28.

17. Ron Lee Davis, *Mentoring: The Strategy of the Master* (Nashville: Thomas Nelson Publishers, 1991), 15.

18. Biehl, xiv.

19. Richard E. Caruso, *Mentoring and the Business Environment: Asset or Liability?* (Aldershot, England: Dartmouth Publishing Company Limited, 1992), 5.

20. Linda K. Johnsrud, "Mentor Relationships: Those That Help and Those That Hinder," *New Directions for Higher Education* 72 (Winter 1990): 62.

21. Martin Gerstein, "Mentoring: An Age Old Practice in a Knowledge-based Society," *Journal of Counseling and Development* 64 (October 1985): 157.

22. Lee Taylor, *Behind the Scrim* (Atlanta, Ga.: Christian Education and Publications, 1991), 43.

23. Bill Lawrence, "Vulnerability: The Primary Ingredient, The Greatest Obstacle," Lecture #8 presented at the Mentoring Conference at Dallas Theological Seminary Center for Christian Leadership, Dallas, Tex., 1991.

24. William H. Stewart, "Who's Ministering to the Youth Minister?" *Plumb Line of Western Seminary*, Spring 1992, p. 1.

25. Colin Brown, ed., *The New International Dictionary of New Testament Theology*, vol. 3, s.v. "diabolos," by H. Bietenhard.

26. Kraft, Vickie, Women Mentoring Women: Ways to Start, Maintain, and Expand a Biblical Women's Ministry (Chicago: Moody Press, 1992), 21.

27. Biehl, 65.

28. Donald M. Joy, *Re-bonding: Preventing and Restoring Damaged Relationships* (Dallas, Tex.: Word Publishers, 1986), 5.

29. Donald M. Joy, *Bonding: Relationships in the Image of God* (Dallas, Tex: Word Publishing, 1985), 108.

30. ibid., 5.

31. Olian et al., "What Do Proteges Look for in a Mentor?" *Journal of Vocational Behavior* 33 (August 1988): 34.

32. Richard H. Tyre, interview in Radnor, Pa., 10 February 1993.

33. ibid.

34. Joy, *Re-Bonding*, 12.

35. Cloud, 46.

36. William H. Stewart, "Who's Ministering to the Youth Minister?" *Plumb Line of Western Seminary*, Spring 1992, 2.

37. S. Merriam, "Mentors and Proteges: A Critical Review of the Literature," *Adult Education Quarterly* 33 (Spring 1983), 161-73.

38. David John Atkinson, *The Message of Ruth: The Wings of Refuge* (Downers Grove, Ill.: Inter-Varsity Press, 1985), 49-50.

39. Robert L. Hubbard, Jr. *Ordinary Faithful People* (Wheaton, Ill.: Victor Books, 1992), 35.

40. Atkinson, 49.

41. Hubbard, 49-50.

42. Kenneth Barker, ed., *The NIV Study Bible: New International Version* (Grand Rapids, Mich.: Zondervan Bible Publishers, 1985), 366.

43. Robert L. Hubbard, Jr. *The Book of Ruth* (Grand Rapids, Mich.: William B. Eerdmans Publishing Company, 1988), 191.

44. Howard and William Hendricks, *As Iron Sharpens Iron* (Chicago: Moody Press, 1995), 116.

45. William J. Petersen, *The Discipling of Timothy* (Wheaton, Ill.: Victor Books Division of SP Publications, Inc., 1980), 166.

46. Walter Bauer, *A Greek-English Lexicon of the New Testament and Other Early Christian Literature*, trans. by William F. Arndt and Wilbur Gingrich, 4th rev. ed. (Chicago, Ill.: The University of Chicago Press, 1957),670.

47. Gerhard Friedrich, ed. *Theological Dictionary of the New Testament*. Translated and edited by Geoffrey W. Bromiley (Grand Rapids, Mich.: Wm. B. Eerdmans Publishing Company, 1972), s.v. "*paratithemi.*"

48. Bauer, 374-75.

49. The word *parakaleo* has a two-sided meaning: (1) to encourage; and (2) to exhort. In the Greek translation of the Old Testament (LXX) *parakaleo* translates the Hebrew *naham* which means to be moved to pity or comfort, to be sorry and to have compassion. The classical Greek emphasizes the meaning of request, entreaty or exhortation (NIDTNT, p. 569, G. Braumann).

50. Robert E. Coleman, *The Master Plan of Evangelism* (Old Tappan, N.J.: Fleming H. Revell Company, 1964), 21.

51. Charles Harold Dodd, *The Interpretation of the Fourth Gospel* (Cambridge, England: University Press, 1954), 183.

52. Leon Morris, *The Gospel According to John* (Grand Rapids, Michigan: Wm. B. Eerdmans Publishing Co., 1971), 335-36.

53. ibid., 158.

54. Iain H. Murray, *Jonathan Edwards: A New Biography* (Carlisle, Penn.: The Banner of Truth Trust, 1987), 179.

55. ibid., 183.

56. Ibid.,182.

57. ibid., 182.

58. ibid., 181.

59. John F. Walvoord, *Philippians: Triumph in Christ* (Chicago: Moody Press, 1971), 70.

60. D. J. Wiseman, ed. *Tyndale Old Testament Commentaries* (Downers Grove, Ill.: InterVarsity Press, 1973), *Exodus*, by R. Alan Cole, 61.

61. ibid., 76.

62. ibid., 138.

63. Richard H. Tyre, "The Seminary of the East: A Questionnaire for Mentors and Mentees," (Radnor, Pa: The Uncommon Individual Foundation Photocopied Notes, 1992), 1-10.

64. William Hendrik Gispen, *Bible Student's Commentary: Exodus*, trans. Ed van de Maas (Grand Rapids, Mich.: Zondervan Publishing House, 1982), 177.

65. Ronald F. Youngblood, *Everyman's Bible Commentary: Exodus* (Chicago: Moody Press, 1983), 89.

66. Gispen, 177.

67. F. B. Huey, *A Study Guide Commentary: Exodus* (Grand Rapids, Mich.: Zondervan Publishing House, 1977), 77.

68. Biehl, 73.

69. Brown, Francis, S.R. Driver, and Charles A. Briggs, *A Hebrew and English Lexicon of the Old Testament* (Oxford: Clarendon Press, 1977), 107.

70. Harris, R. Laird, Gleason L. Archer, and Bruce Waltke, eds., *Theological Workbook of the Old Testament*, vol. 2 (Chicago: Moody Press, 1980), s.v. "*sharat*," by Herman J. Austel.

71. Peter Deison, *Mentoring* (Dallas, Tex.: Dallas Theological Seminary Tape Ministry, 1992), tape no. 2.

72. U. Cassuto, *A Commentary on the Book of Exodus* (Jerusalem: The Magnes Press, 1983), 206.

73. Billy Graham, *JUST AS I AM: The Autobiography of Billy Graham* (New York: HarperCollins Publishers, 1997), 47.

74. ibid., 47.

75. ibid., 48.

76. ibid., 48-49.

77. ibid., 58.

78. Barker, 514.

79. Harris, s.v. "*mashah.*

80. *Theological Wordbook of the Old Testament*, vol. 2, s.v. "*sharat,*" by Hermann J. Austel.

81. Frank E. Gaebelein, ed. *The Expositor's Bible Commentary* (Grand Rapids, Mich.: Zondervan Publishing House, 1988) vol. 4, *1, 2 Kings*, by Richard D. Patterson and Hermann J. Austel, 175.

82. Fee, 143.

83. Fee, 143.

84. Stanley and Clinton, *Connecting*, 171.

85. Stanley and Clinton, *Connecting*, 192.

86. Sidney M. Jourard, *Self-Disclosure: An Experimental Analysis of the Transparent Self* (New York: John Wiley and Sons, Inc., 1971), 13.

87. Edward C. Sellner, *Mentoring: The Ministry of Spiritual Kinship* (Notre Dame, Ind.: Ave Maria Press, 1990), 54.

88. Walter Bauer, *A Greek-English Lexicon of the New Testament and Other Early Christian Literature*, trans. by William F. Arndt and Wilbur Gingrich, 4th rev. ed. (Chicago, Ill.: The University of Chicago Press, 1957), 64.

89. Frank E. Gaebelein, ed. *The Expositor's Bible Commentary* (Grand Rapids, Mich.: Zondervan Publishing House, 1978), vol. 11, *Ephesians-Philemon*, by Ralph Earle, 364.

90. Bauer, 583.

91. Gaebelein, *First Timothy*, 11:363.

92. W. Ward Gasque, ed., *A Good News Commentary* (San Francisco: Harper and Row, Publishers, 1984), *First and Second Timothy, Titus*, by Gordon D. Fee, 42-43.

93. Leith Anderson, *Dying for Change* (Minneapolis, Minn.: Bethany House Publishers, 1990), 52-57.

94. James Keating, "The Religion Teacher as Mentor-Friend," *Momentum* 15 (December 1984): 32.

95. William Barclay, *The Letters to Timothy, Titus, and Philemon* (Philadelphia: Westminster, 1975), 83.

96. Gene A. Getz, *The Measure of a Man* (Ventura, Calif.: Regal Books, 1974), 38.

97. Bauer, 809.

98. Gerhard Kittel, ed. *Theological Dictionary of the New Testament*, trans. and ed. by Geoffrey W. Bromley (Grand Rapids, Mich.: Wm. B. Eerdmans Publishing Company, 1965), "kosmios," by H. Sasse.

99. Getz, 65.

100. Marsha Playko, "What It Means to be Mentored," *NASSP Bulletin* 74 (May 1990): 30.

101. Knowles, 1ff.

102. Paul Stanley and Bobby Clinton, "Up, Sideways, Down: The Network You Need to Succeed," *Discipleship Journal* 68 (Spring 1992): 61.

CPSIA information can be obtained at www.ICGtesting.com
Printed in the USA
BVOW032218040113

309793BV00005B/9/P

9 781624 197321